Horizons

Geography 11–14

1

David Gardner

Roger Knill

John Smith

Published in 2004 by:
Nelson Thornes Ltd
Delta Place
27 Bath Road
CHELTENHAM
GL53 7TH
United Kingdom

04 05 06 07 08 / 10 9 8 7 6 5 4 3 2 1

A catalogue record for this book is available from the British Library

ISBN 0 7487 9049 7

Illustrations by Gordon Lawson, Richard Morris, David Russell Illustration

Page make-up by eMC Design, www.emcdesign.org.uk

Printed in Croatia by Zrinski

Horizons PB 1 Acknowledgements

Acestock: p.108A; Art Directors and TRIP Photo Library: p.31A; Associated Press:
pp.64/65 C-F, 78 (both pictures), 79, 83 (picture 4); John Birdsall: p.109E; Mark Boulton:
pp.94/95D, 109D; Brendan Byrne/ Digital Vision 5D (NT): p.118; Michael Cole/ Dunlop
Slazenger: p.96C; Corbis/ C/B Productions: p.31B; Corbis/ Charles & Josette Lenars:
p.37D (top); Corbis/ Charles Gupton: 100A; Corbis/ Dallas and John Heaton: p105H;
Corbis/ Galen Rowell: p.27B (top middle); Corbis/ Jason Hawkes: p.125 (top right);
Corbis/ Johnathan Smith/ Cordaiy Photo Library Ltd: p.104E; Corbis/ Owaki-Kulla: p.4B;
Corbis/ Richard Morrell: p.87F; Corbis/ Vince Streano: pp.34/35A; Corbis/ WildCountry:
pp.16/17B; Corel 138 (NT): 37D (top left); Corel 186 (NT): p.104F; Corel 236 (NT): p.27B
(middle bottom); Corel 292 (NT): pp.4C, 124 (middle right); Corel 361 (NT): p.57C; Corel
485 (NT): p.27B (upper middle); Corel 640 (NT): p.60B; Digital Stock 7 (NT): p.86D; Digital
Vision 1 (NT): front cover; Digital Vision 7 (NT): p.13G; Environment Agency: pp.64B, 73C,
75B, 75C; David Gardner: pp.11A (top), 14/15A, 19B, 19C, 19D, 22/23A, 23B, 22/23C,
23D, 23E, 69B, 69C, 72B, 72F, 73D, 83C (pictures 1, 3, 6, 7, 8, 10); Geophotos: p.27B (top
left); Get Mapping: pp.6A, 8A, 8B; Getty Images: pp.25B, 56B, 87G; Holt Studios: p.27B
(bottom right); Eric & David Hosking: pp.4/5A, 124 (top); Hutchison Library: pp.17C, 36A;
Imperial War Museum: p.108B; Infoterra: front cover resource A; Roger Knill: pp.38A, 42B,
42C; London Aerial Photo Library: p.125 (left); Mary Evans Picture Library/ Peter Stokoe:
p.90A; MODIS Rapid Response Project at NASA/ GSFC: p.77A; naturepl.com/ Gavin
Hellier: pp.105G, 124 (bottom right); naturepl.com/ Lynn Stone: p.27B (lower middle);
Øivind Leren/ Norsk Hydro: p.94B; PA Photos: p.83C (pictures 2 and 9); Panos Pictures/
Fred Hoogervorst: p.80D; Photodisc 22 (NT): p.104C; Photodisc 31 (NT): p.27B (bottom
left); photos.com: pp.102 (bottom), 105A, 124 (main); Rex: p.37D (bottom pictures);
Sebastiao Salgado/ Amazonas/ nbpictures: pp.24/25A; John Smith: pp.44A, 44B, 45C,
48A, 50B, 51C, 51D, 51E, 52A, 53D, 54E, 58B, 60A, 60C, 61D, 85 (upper and lower middle
and bottom), 88B, 88D, 90 (bottom), 91B (all pictures), 92A, 93D; Will Smith: p.85 (top);
Still Pictures: pp.87H, 81E; Sunset Avenue Productions/ Digital Vision WA (NT): pp.58A,
125 (middle right); Enok Sweetland: p.39B; Topham Picturepoint: pp.86C, 87E; Simon
Warner: p.59C; www.jasonhawkes.com: p.27B (top right), 104B, 104D;
www.petersmith.com: pp.70A, 73E; York & County Press: pp.64A, 71C.

Maps produced from Ordnance Survey mapping with the permission of the Controller
of Her Majesty's Stationery Office. © Crown copyright. All rights reserved. Licence
No.100017284: front cover resource B, back cover resource E, and pp.10B, 40B, 92B,
125 (top).

contents

Where are we going?

In this unit you will find out about your new secondary school and its locality. You will use the geographical skills and understanding of places that you developed in your primary school.

You will also learn about:

- **the connections between places around the world**
- **how these places are connected to places that you know**
- **how to describe places**
- **how to locate places**
- **how to conduct an enquiry.**

The Grand **A** Canyon, USA – voted the most popular place to see in your lifetime

When you studied Geography at primary school, which places did you study?

The BBC Holiday website recently asked users to tell them about the places they think that everyone should see in their lifetime. People voted for places and the BBC compiled a top 50 list which you can see on the website. Three of the most popular places were the Grand Canyon (**A**), New York City (**B**) and Windermere (**C**).

New York **B** City, USA – voted the most popular city to see

C Windermere – voted the most popular place in the UK

WEBLINKS You will find a link to the BBC Holiday website at www.nelsonthornes.com/horizons/weblinks

Where is this place?

What is it like?

Why is it like this?

What do I feel about the place?

How is it changing?

Who is affected by these changes?

OVER TO YOU

1 The areas shown in photos **A**, **B** and **C** were voted the 'most popular places to see'. Choose one of the photos.
 a Describe what you can see in that picture. Use the key questions above photo **A** to help you.
 b What do you think made people vote for that place?

2 Now choose one of the other photos.
 a Describe that place.
 b Why do you think people voted for that place?
 c Compare the two places that you have described in activities 1 and 2. Try to say if they are the same in some ways and why they are different in others.

3 Does your class agree with the choice of places voted for on the BBC website? Conduct your own class survey.
 a Each pupil in your class can vote for five places to see in your lifetime. You could also conduct the survey for cities or places in the United Kingdom.
 b Once everyone has voted, collect the results.
 c Write a list of the places voted for. Keep a score of the number of votes for each place.
 d Produce a list in rank order to show which are the most popular places voted by your class.
 e Now draw a bar graph to show the places and the number of votes for each one.

4 People have different feelings about places. Here are two views about the Grand Canyon:

'It is the most amazing place on Earth – vast, overwhelming, overpowering, very spiritual. Makes you feel so small and insignificant. With all the power of modern technology it just reminds you that nature is stronger and more powerful.'
Sue Washer, Cardiff

'Been there – not that exciting. Just a big hole! Drove for 6/7 hours – big hole – got back in car and drove back.'
Jeremy Edwards

Look at photo **A** again. Which opinion do you agree with? Explain why you agree with it.

What is the number of my place?

Congratulations! You have just started your new secondary school.

- **Where is it?**
- **What is it like?**

As you now know from pages 4 and 5, these are just two of the questions geographers ask. In particular, geographers are interested in location. At your primary school you investigated the location of places. See if you can apply this work to your new school by finding out its grid reference numbers.

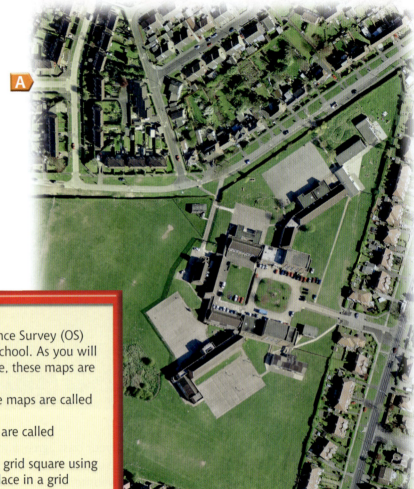

A

Help!

Using grid references

You may already have used an Ordnance Survey (OS) map for geography work at your primary school. As you will remember, to help you locate where places are, these maps are provided with a grid of numbered lines.

- The lines from the top to the bottom of the maps are called *eastings*.
- Lines running horizontally across the maps are called *northings*.

These lines create grid squares. You can find a grid square using four-figure grid references. You can locate a place in a grid square by using a six-figure grid reference.

B Using grid references

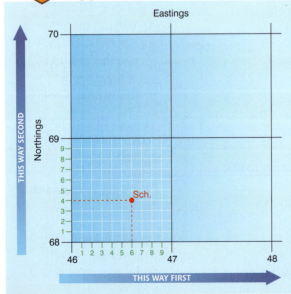

1 Grid lines 46 and 68 cross at the bottom left-hand corner of the grid square in which the school in photo **A** is found. The four-figure grid reference of the school is 4668. The easting is always given first and then the northing.

2 To be more accurate, imagine that the sides of each grid square are divided into tenths.

3 To find the school, start at easting 46 and count how many tenths across towards easting 47 it is. Write down the easting number followed by the number of tenths – 466.

4 Then look up the side of the square starting at northing 68. The school is four-tenths of the way to northing 69. Write down the northing number followed by the number of tenths – 684.

5 This is written as 466684. This is called a six-figure grid reference.

A similar system to grid references is used to find any place on the Earth's surface. The best way to show the whole of the Earth is on a globe, which is three-dimensional. Look at a globe in your classroom. To help you locate a place on the globe, a grid of lines has been provided.

Lines of **latitude** are imaginary horizontal lines running around the Earth from east to west. The line around the middle of the Earth is called the equator. Latitude is measured in degrees to the north and south of the equator, which is 0 degrees. Any place not on the equator must be either north or south of it. The highest latitudes are the North Pole at 90ºN and the South Pole at 90ºS.

Lines of **longitude** are imaginary vertical lines which run from north to south. They are measured from the Greenwich (or Prime) Meridian which is 0 degrees. All places that are not on this line must be either east or west of it.

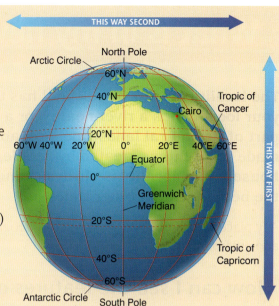

C

The main lines of latitude and longitude

The space between each line of latitude and longitude is divided into 60 smaller parts called minutes. When you locate a place using latitude and longitude, give the latitude number first. For example, Cairo in Egypt is 30º03′N and 31º15′E.

The Royal Mail uses postcodes to locate places. Everywhere in the United Kingdom has one. A postcode identifies a group of houses or addresses and is designed to help with the automated sorting of mail.

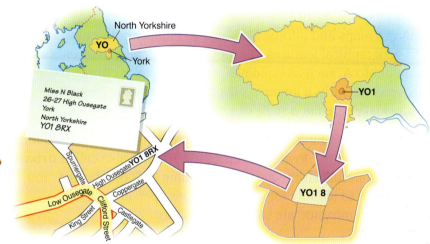

D

How postcodes work

Find the information you need to complete a copy of table **E**. You can find out the numbers using the following things:

- an Ordnance Survey map of your local area

- an atlas

- your new school's pupil planner or prospectus.

The place	Numbers/letters
The four-figure grid reference of my new school	
The six-figure grid reference of my new school	
The four-figure grid reference of my old school	
The six-figure grid reference of my old school	
The four-figure grid reference of my home	
The six-figure grid reference of my home	
The latitude and longitude for my school (find the nearest town or city that is listed in the index of your atlas)	
The postcode of my new school	
The postcode of my house	

E

The numbers of my places

What is in my new locality?

The locality of your new school has unique features. If your locality has a river nearby, or a steep slope, this is part of its natural landscape. Probably much of the area is made up of things created by people, such as roads and houses. Your locality is always changing, sometimes for the better – and at other times not.

Any place is a mixture of three types of geography: physical, human and environmental.

How can I see the features of a locality?

Maps and vertical aerial photos show the features of a place or locality. Photo **A** is a vertical aerial photo of York. It shows the same area as the OS map shown on the back cover resource **E**. Both the photo and the map are at the same scale.

You can use maps and photos like these to identify both physical and human geographical features. It is possible to identify different **land uses** on photo **A**, such as buildings, roads and fields. To see these features more clearly, a larger-scale photo is required. Photo **B** shows a smaller area at a scale of 1:5000.

The city of York is a built-up area, where most of the land is used for housing and industry. Towns and cities like this are also called **urban** areas. Look carefully at the areas surrounding York on photo **A**. You should be able to identify lots of fields. More open areas like these in the countryside are called **rural** areas.

C

Feature	Name of feature
Village A	
Museum B	
Building C	
Leisure facility D	
Building E	
Natural area F	
River G	
Road H	

OVER TO YOU

1 Write the meanings of these phrases in your own words:
- physical geography
- human geography
- environmental geography.

2 Look at this list of topics:
  a Studying how rivers wear away the sides of their valley
  b Learning why the rainforest needs to be protected
  c Looking at a farmer's work in different seasons
  d Predicting volcanoes
  e Saving the whale

  f The types of housing in different parts of a town.
  Which topics are physical geography? Which are human geography? Which are environmental geography?

3 Eight features are marked on photo **A** with letters. Find those features on the photo and also on the OS map of York on back cover resource **E**. Use information from the map and photo to fill in a copy of table **C**.

4 Write a list of land uses for the area around the school shown in photo **B**.

5 a You can find similar maps and vertical aerial photos for the area around your school on the internet.

  Enter the postcode of your school in the 'Quicksearch/Find' box on the Multimap website, and select the correct scale.

  b Write a list of land uses for the area around your school.

WEBLINKS You will find a link to Multimap at www.nelsonthornes.com/horizons/weblinks

Vertical aerial photo of part of the west of York –
see the back cover resource **E**. The school at
566508 is very clear on this photo.

How can I draw a field sketch?

Field sketching is an important geographical skill when conducting fieldwork. You need to look carefully at a landscape and decide which geographical features should be drawn and labelled.

You do not have to be good at drawing, but you do need to develop the skill of identifying geographical features to draw. Field sketches are best drawn from a place with a view, such as the top of a hill or tall building.

Drawing a field sketch is a great way to record the geographical features in your new school locality. It is useful to have an Ordnance Survey map with you to help you identify the features.

All Year 7 pupils at Raincliffe School in Scarborough draw a field sketch of their new locality soon after starting at the school. Their teachers help them to produce it in stages (diagram **A**). They also use an OS map (map **B**).

OVER TO YOU

1 Use sketch **A** and map **B** to help you to complete the title for this field sketch:

A field sketch of Raincliffe School and its locality from H_____ Hill, grid reference _____ looking in a _____ direction.

2 Look at the final field sketch and the OS map. Name the following features:

a the type or class of road at A

b area of housing B

c building C

d the type or class of road at D

e building E

f area of housing F

g building G in the distance

h building H

i building I.

3 Why do you think the map is turned on its side?

4 a Enter the postcode for Raincliffe School – YO12 5RL – in the 'Quicksearch/Find' box on the Multimap website.

WEBLINKS You will find a link to Multimap at www.nelsonthornes.com/horizons/weblinks

b Once a map of the school has downloaded, change the scale to 1:10 000 and switch to an aerial photo.

c Copy and paste the aerial photo of Raincliffe School into a desktop publishing file, or print it out.

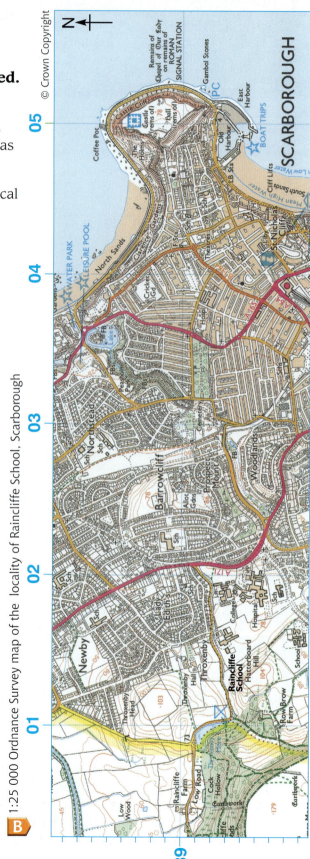

1:25 000 Ordnance Survey map of the locality of Raincliffe School, Scarborough

B

A

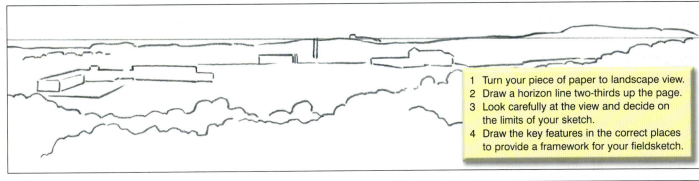

The first stage is to look carefully at the view and pick out the key features with the use of the OS map.

1 Turn your piece of paper to landscape view.
2 Draw a horizon line two-thirds up the page.
3 Look carefully at the view and decide on the limits of your sketch.
4 Draw the key features in the correct places to provide a framework for your fieldsketch.

Add more detail to your sketch.

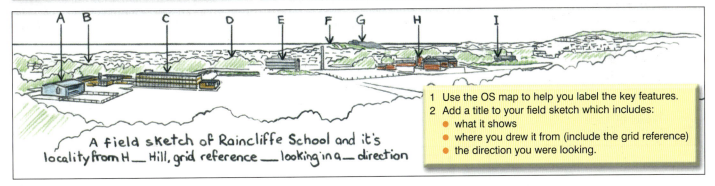

A field sketch of Raincliffe School and it's locality from H___ Hill, grid reference ___ looking in a ___ direction

1 Use the OS map to help you label the key features.
2 Add a title to your field sketch which includes:
  ● what it shows
  ● where you drew it from (include the grid reference)
  ● the direction you were looking.

d Label different land uses on your aerial photo. You will find it useful to refer to diagram **A** and map **B**.

5 Draw a field sketch of your school and its locality. Look for a high point from where you can draw your sketch. Discuss this with your teacher. You may not have a nearby hill as at Raincliffe School, but you could draw your sketch from a classroom window. You will need a sheet of paper, pen, pencil, eraser and an Ordnance Survey map of your locality, at a scale of either 1:50 000 or 1:25 000. Use the map to help you identify the key geographical features to label on your sketch.

6 **Homework** Draw a field sketch of the area around your house. Again look for a high point from which to draw your sketch. Make sure that it is safe – perhaps one of your parents can go with you. They may have useful local knowledge of the area that could help with your labelling.

Where do I live?

You know the address of your home, but do you know your world address? Jacob is a Year 7 pupil at Raincliffe School in Scarborough. He lives very close to his new school at Throxenby Lane, Scarborough YO12 5RL. But his world address is much longer – like all of us he is a citizen of planet Earth ...

Fantastic Facts

There are over 260 countries in the world. Imagine how long it would take you to visit them all!

OVER TO YOU

1 Maps **A–G** show the world address for Jacob. Match each map or image with one of the words in the boxes below.

locality **planet** **town**

county **country**

kingdom **continent**

2 The maps and images are arranged in order of size, starting with the smallest. This is how you write an address.
  a Write the world address for Jacob.
  b Write your own world address.

3 A good geographer knows about places and where they are. Let's see how much you know! Name:
  a the countries that make up the United Kingdom
  b the four capital cities in the United Kingdom
  c the physical geography features A–E on map **E**
  d the capital cities marked on map **F**
  e the seas labelled A–D on map **F**
  f the continents and ocean labelled 1–4 on image **G**.

The front cover resource **C** of the British Isles, and the back cover resource **F** of the world, will help you.

D England, population 49 million

C North Yorkshire, population 570 000

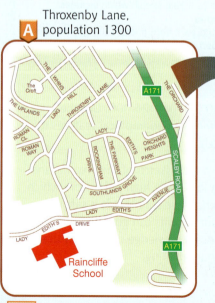

A Throxenby Lane, population 1300

B Scarborough, population 52 000

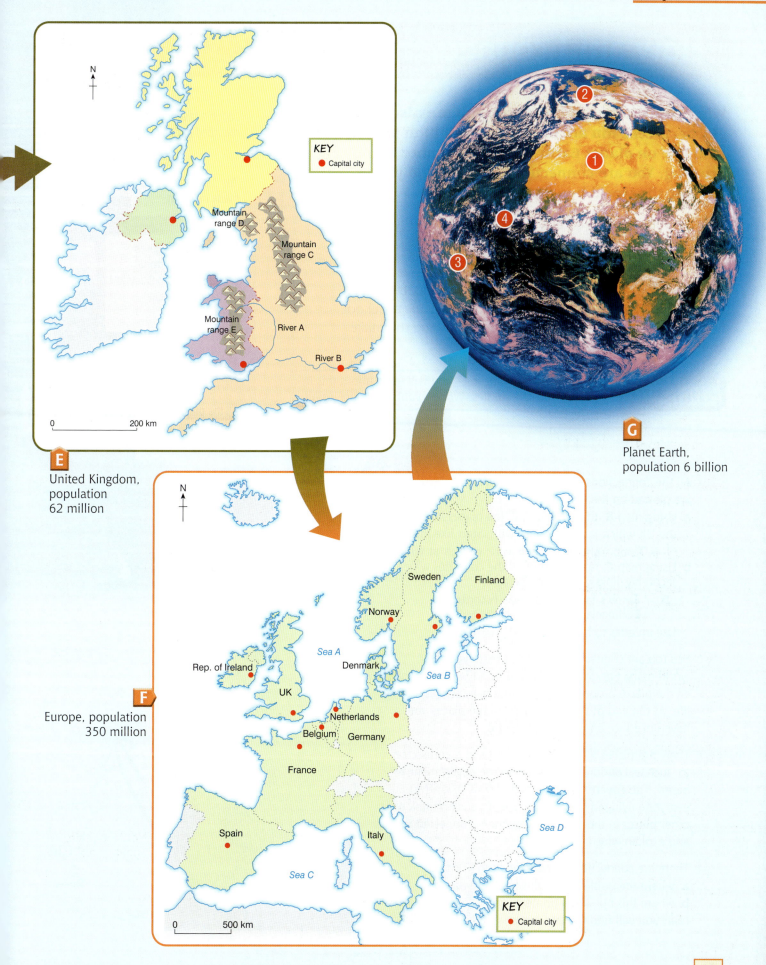

KEY
● Capital city

Mountain range D
Mountain range C
Mountain range E
River A
River B

0   200 km

E United Kingdom, population 62 million

G Planet Earth, population 6 billion

F Europe, population 350 million

N

Sweden
Finland
Norway
Sea A
Rep. of Ireland
Denmark
Sea B
UK
Netherlands
Belgium
Germany
France
Sea D
Spain
Italy
Sea C

0   500 km

KEY
● Capital city

How am I connected to places?

Wherever you live in the world, you are also a *global citizen*. You are one of over 6 billion people who live on planet Earth – and the number is growing. You are connected to people and places all over the world in a variety of ways.

Photo **A** shows Jacob alone in his bedroom in Scarborough, but even here he is connected to people and places all over the world.

Maps **B** and **C** show the connections made by Jacob in his bedroom. He makes many more in his everyday life at school, in the food he eats and in the places he visits. You too make connections around the world every day.

Links to... We are all global citizens – you will learn about this in your Citizenship studies. World events influence us all.

1 All the connections shown on photo **A** are plotted on the two maps.
  a Using map **B**, make a list of all the places in the UK which Jacob has links with. Start like this:
    1 = Jacob visited the *Endeavour* replica at Whitby.
  b Using map **C**, make a list of all the countries which Jacob has links with. Start like this:
    A = Jacob's favourite CD was recorded in California, USA.
  Use an atlas to help you.

2 You too are connected to places. Create your own world diary. For one week keep a list in your diary of all the places around the world that have touched your life. At the end of the week show all the places you have linked to, on maps like **B** and **C**.

3 There are places in the UK that everyone is connected to, such as London which is where the government is based. The government makes decisions that affect everyone living in the country. See if you can think of other places in the UK that everyone is connected to, and explain why.

4 There are connections in **Horizons** too. Find out:
  a where the publishers of this book are based
  b where this book was printed.
  Hint: you will find the answers on page 2.

Jacob's favourite CD was recorded in California.

The playstation was made in Japan.

The terracotta figures were a present from Jacob's aunt's holiday to China. She lives in Sheffield.

A

All the playstation games were made in Austria.

B

0   50 km

N

Scarborough

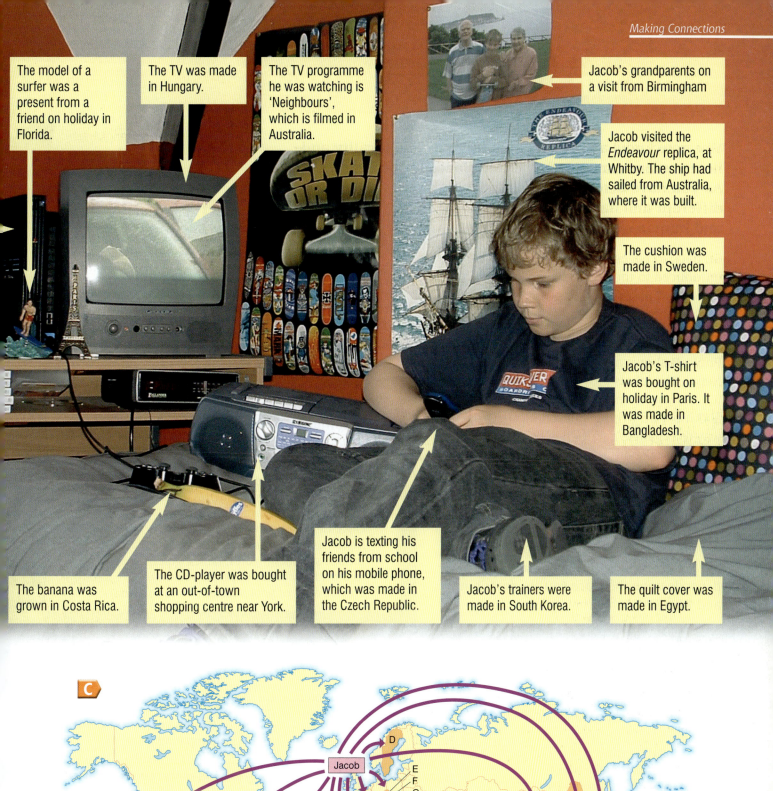

The model of a surfer was a present from a friend on holiday in Florida.

The TV was made in Hungary.

The TV programme he was watching is 'Neighbours', which is filmed in Australia.

Jacob's grandparents on a visit from Birmingham

Jacob visited the *Endeavour* replica, at Whitby. The ship had sailed from Australia, where it was built.

The cushion was made in Sweden.

Jacob's T-shirt was bought on holiday in Paris. It was made in Bangladesh.

The banana was grown in Costa Rica.

The CD-player was bought at an out-of-town shopping centre near York.

Jacob is texting his friends from school on his mobile phone, which was made in the Czech Republic.

Jacob's trainers were made in South Korea.

The quilt cover was made in Egypt.

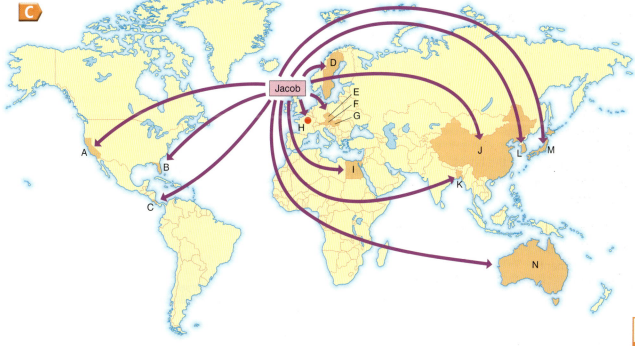

How can I write about places?

You now know a great deal about your new locality and how you are connected to other places around the world. As you have discovered, all places are different and have their own physical and human geographical features.

Go back to pages 4 and 5. Here you were introduced to the key questions geographers ask about places. A good geographer uses these as part of a toolkit of things to do when describing a place.

Help!

You will find the toolkit below very useful throughout your studies in Geography. Get into the routine of using it. It will help you to become a much better geographer.

Nepal

B

Photo **B** shows a scene in the foothills of Nepal. The labels provide geographical terms (words) and questions for you to think about before writing a description. A good way to organise a written description of a place is to set out this list of geographical terms and write a few sentences about them. Make sure you use the describing toolkit **A**. Try to give evidence to back up your answers to the questions shown on photo **B**, and explain the points you make. You do not always have to use the same terms – it depends upon the place you are describing and whether each term is relevant to it.

A

A geographer's describing toolkit

- Ask key questions.
- Be accurate.
- Research information, using books, atlases, newspapers, CD-ROMs, the internet.
- Use geographical terms (words).
- Organise your writing into paragraphs.
- *Explain* as well as *describe* a place.
- Include statistics (figures, tables, graphs, maps), to provide evidence of points you make.
- Provide a list of your sources of information.

OVER TO YOU

1 Look at photo **B**. To write a geographer's description of this place you need to answer some of the questions written round the edge of the photo.
  a Start by answering the questions in the boxes headed:
  - Location
  - Relief.
  b Then try to answer the boxes headed:
  - Climate
  - Vegetation.
  c Then look at the boxes:
  - Population
  - Settlement
  - Work.

  d Then look at the Drainage and Communications boxes. Now write a Conclusion to complete your description.

2 Photo **C** shows an area of Bangladesh. Write a description of this scene. Choose some of the questions around photo **B** to help you. *Hint:* Drainage and

Work will be important boxes for this photo.

3 Each place in the world is unique (different). Comparing places can help you identify differences and similarities between places. Diagram **D** is a **Venn diagram**. You can use a diagram like this to compare two places. This diagram has been partly completed, comparing photos **B** and **C**.

Features unique to this place	Features similar in each place	Features unique to this place
Steep mountains	South East Asia	Flat lowlands
Nepal		**Bangladesh**

D

Location
- Where is this place?
- What is its latitude and longitude?

Relief
- What is the height and shape of the land?
- Is it steep, gently sloping or flat?

Drainage
- What water features, such as rivers, streams and lakes, can you see?

Population
- How many people live in the area?
- Does it seem crowded or empty?

Settlement
- Where do people live?
- Are there villages or towns, or just scattered farms?

Climate
- What evidence can you see of high or low temperatures or rainfall?
- Find out the average temperatures and rainfall from an atlas.

Vegetation
- What plant life can you see?
- Is there forest, grassland or farmland?

Communications
- What methods of travel seem to be available?
- Does travel seem to be easy or difficult?

Work
- What sorts of jobs will people do for a living?

Conclusion
- Summarise what the place is like. What do you think about the place?

a Make your own larger copy of diagram **D**.
b Complete it using your descriptions from activities 1 and 2.
c Write a paragraph comparing photos **B** and **C**.

4 a Write a description of your local area, using the list of geographical terms provided with photo **B** to help you.
b Complete another Venn diagram to compare your local area with *either* photo **B** *or* photo **C**.
c Write a paragraph comparing the two places.

C Bangladesh farming landscape

How do I conduct an enquiry? Part 1

In this unit you have been asking questions about places. These questions can often be answered through an enquiry or investigation. Geographical enquiry is a process, similar to scientific investigation. Hopefully you are familiar with it already. It is a bit like being a detective involving:

- asking key questions
- collecting, presenting and analysing evidence
- coming to a conclusion from your findings.

When you conduct an enquiry there are a number of steps for you to follow, as shown in diagram **A**.

In the next few pages you will learn about these steps and conduct an enquiry of your own.

Primary evidence

This is information you find for yourself by visiting the place and conducting surveys. This is called **fieldwork**.

Secondary evidence

This information can be collected without visiting the place. Use sources such as books, maps and newspapers, or use ICT such as the internet or CD-ROMs.

Links to... The enquiry process is very important in Geography and Science. You will conduct investigations in both subjects many times in your future studies. It is important that you understand this process.

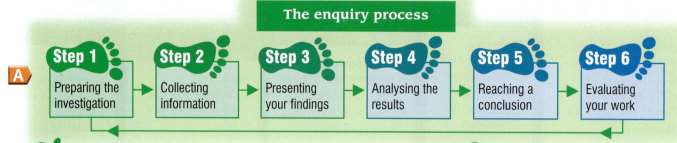

The enquiry process

A

Step 1 Preparing the investigation → **Step 2** Collecting information → **Step 3** Presenting your findings → **Step 4** Analysing the results → **Step 5** Reaching a conclusion → **Step 6** Evaluating your work

Step 1
Preparing the investigation

The first thing you need to do is decide what and where it is you are going to investigate. An easy place to investigate would be your school.

There are many different types of geographical enquiry. Some enquiries can investigate an issue or problem that affects people, others can be used to test an idea.

Many issues in Geography are to do with the environment. It can easily be spoilt or damaged if it is not looked after. All teachers and pupils at your school should be concerned about the school environment, so this would be a useful theme to investigate.

All enquiries begin with a **key question**. Answering this question is the aim of your enquiry. Here are some ideas:

- How environmentally friendly is our school?
- Is there a litter problem at our new school?

It is better if you think up your own key question to investigate.

Step 2
Collecting information

Once you have decided on your key question, you need to decide how you are going to answer it. You can collect both primary and secondary evidence. Collecting information is best done at the actual place, but this is not always possible.

In this enquiry you have easy access to your study area (school!), so all of your information can be collected by fieldwork.

One very useful form of survey used by geographers is to record images of the study area. This can be done by drawing field sketches or by taking photos. Photos **B**, **C** and **D** were taken at a school using a digital camera. This type of camera is very useful when conducting fieldwork because you can look at your picture instantly, then delete or retake shots as necessary.

How to carry out this survey

An environmental quality survey can be used to measure the quality of a place. Diagram **E** is a survey sheet for an investigation of a school.

1   Look carefully at your survey location. On a copy of diagram **E**, record where it is, and the date of the survey.

2   Award points for each feature shown on the survey sheet. If a place is very attractive it will score 5 points; if it is ugly it will score 1 point; if it is somewhere in between it will score 2, 3 or 4 points.

3   Place a tick ✔ in one of the columns to give that point's score for each feature. You will need to discuss the points to award with other members of your group.

4   When you have completed the survey, add up the total score for your location. The higher the total the better the quality of the environment.

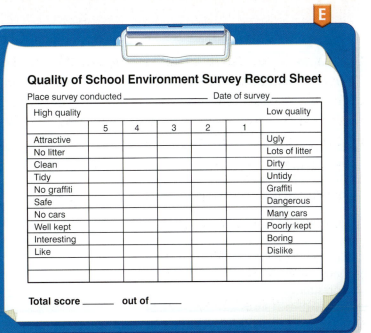

E

Quality of School Environment Survey Record Sheet

Place survey conducted _____   Date of survey _____

High quality	5	4	3	2	1	Low quality
Attractive						Ugly
No litter						Lots of litter
Clean						Dirty
Tidy						Untidy
No graffiti						Graffiti
Safe						Dangerous
No cars						Many cars
Well kept						Poorly kept
Interesting						Boring
Like						Dislike

Total score _____ **out of** _____

B This photo was taken at point X on map **A** page 20

This photo was taken at point Y on map **A** page 20 **C**

D This photo was taken at point Z on map **A** page 20

OVER TO YOU

1 a Describe what photos **B**, **C** and **D** show about the school. *Hint*: Look for litter.
   b The pupils selected these locations. Do you think they portray a balanced view of the school environment or a biased view?
   c On copies of diagram **E**, record scores for each location shown in photos **B**, **C** and **D**.

2 Conduct an environmental survey of your own school.
   a Your class can be divided into groups. Each group selects a different location to conduct their survey.
   b Plot these locations on a school plan.
   c As a class, discuss how you will score the survey. Diagram **E** has two extra rows for you to add other things to score.
   d Complete your survey at your chosen location. You can also draw a field sketch or take a picture of your site to provide evidence to support your scores.

How do I conduct an enquiry? Part 2

Step 3

Presenting your findings

Once you have collected all your data, you need to present the results. They need to clearly show patterns and distributions. Diagrams **A** and **B** show two different ways that a class decided to present the results of their school environment survey. They also produced a neat version of their field sketches for each location, and annotated (labelled) their photos to help explain the scores they gave for each location.

Help!

Presenting the results of an investigation is a very important geographical skill. You always need to present work clearly, neatly and accurately. Remember to add a title so that it is clear what is being presented.

Step 4

Analysing the results

This is where you write about what your results show. For each set of data that you have presented you will need to write at least a paragraph to describe and explain what it shows. The toolkit on page 16 will help you with this.

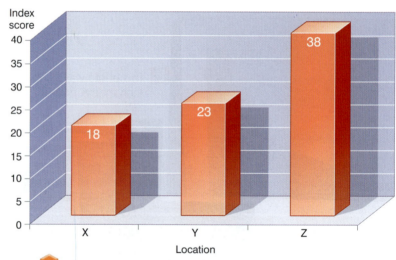

A

KEY
Buildings

B School environment quality survey results. The points X, Y and Z can be seen in photos **B**, **C** and **D** on page 19.

1 Which of the two presentation techniques shown in diagrams **A** and **B** do you think is the most useful in identifying patterns in the quality of the school environment?

2 Compare your scores in activity 2 on page 19 with the final scores recorded on diagram **A**. Are they similar or different? If they are different, can you explain why?

3 If you have conducted a similar survey of your school, present your findings using a variety of techniques.

4 Write up the results *either* for your school survey *or* using those in diagram **A**. Use writing frame **C** to help you.

OVER TO YOU

C

My class conducted an environmental survey of our school grounds on _____

We added _____ to the survey sheet because _____

_____

We experienced the following problems when conducting the survey:

_____

_____

The survey shows that there is a variety in the environmental quality of the school grounds.

The places with the highest-quality environment are _____

_____

The places with the lowest-quality environment are _____

_____

The three best features of the school grounds are _____

_____

_____

The three worst features of the school grounds are _____

_____

_____

This environmental survey has shown that the school has a number of environmental problems.

These are _____

_____

Step 5

Reaching a conclusion

It is here that you pull together all the findings of your investigation. You begin the conclusion by looking back at your key question (Step 1 on page 18). Using the evidence you have collected, answer the key question. If your enquiry has investigated a problem or issue, in the conclusion you can suggest solutions based on your evidence.

Step 6

Evaluating your work

This is the final part of your enquiry, where you review the whole investigation. Here you identify the strengths and weaknesses of your work and suggest improvements in the way the enquiry was conducted.

5 Write a conclusion *either* for your school survey *or* using the results shown in diagrams **A** and **B**. In your conclusion you should:

- Begin by stating your key question.
- Summarise the findings of the fieldwork.
- Describe and explain the environment score.
- Make an overall comment about the quality of the school environment.
- Suggest ways that the school environment can be improved.

6 Identify the strengths of the school environment survey by answering the following questions:

a What do you consider was the most useful or important aspect of the investigation?

b Which surveys do you think were successful?

7 Identify the weaknesses of the school environment survey by answering the following questions:

a What problems did you experience in conducting the enquiry?

b Would your results and conclusions be more meaningful if you had conducted more or different surveys?

8 Suggest ideas for further investigations of your school environment.

Help! The conclusion is the most important part of the enquiry. If you can produce clear and detailed conclusions that are linked to your findings, you will achieve higher levels in Geography.

Making Connections

This unit has helped you to settle into your new secondary school in two ways:

1 by investigating your school to help you find your way around

2 by finding out how talented you are as a geographer.

In this unit you have learned:

- how to describe places
- how to locate places
- how to conduct an enquiry.

Let's see how successful you have been.

A The River Ouse taken from a bridge on the outer ring road A1237.

Clue: Look closely at the building in the background – it will help you to work out which direction the camera was pointing.

OVER TO YOU

Each photo on this spread shows a place in York or its surrounding area. This area is also shown on the OS map on back cover resource **E**.

1 Look carefully at each photo and then attempt the following:

a Compare each photo **A–E** with the OS map of York on back cover resource **E**. Use the evidence in each photo to find the four-figure or six-figure grid reference for the place where you think the

photo was taken from. There is a clue for each photo to help you.

b Which direction was the camera pointing when each photo was taken?

2 a Make a larger copy of table **F**.

b Complete the table by finding geographical features in each photo and listing them in the correct column.

3 Write a geographical description for one of the photos.

Clue: A railway station named after a village on the north-western edge of York. **C**

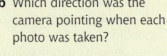
Let's discuss Remember the key questions you learned to ask about places (page 4), With a partner, answer the six key questions about any one of these photos **A–E**.

F

Photo	List physical geography features evident in the photo	List human geography features evident in the photo	List different land uses you can see in the photo	Record whether the photo is showing an urban or a rural scene
A				
B				
C				
D				
E				

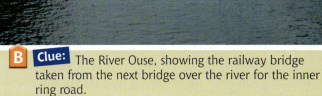

B **Clue:** The River Ouse, showing the railway bridge taken from the next bridge over the river for the inner ring road.

Clue: The large building in the distance is York Minster. The photo was taken from the top of Clifford's Tower (marked as 'Castle' on the OS map).
E

Clue: On the OS map find the road junctions
D shown on this road sign.

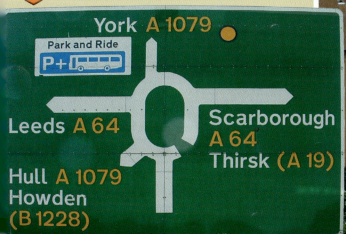

York A 1079
Park and Ride
P + 🚌
Leeds A 64
Scarborough A 64
Thirsk (A 19)
Hull A 1079
Howden (B 1228)

2 People

Can the world cope?

Where are we going?

In this unit you will learn about people.

- **What is the world's total population?**
- **How does population change?**
- **Who is affected by population change?**
- **Where do people move and why?**
- **Why do people live where they live?**
- **Why do settlements grow and change?**

Take a good look at photos **A** and **B**. For each one, ask yourself, 'What has this got to do with me?' Try to ask the same question from different viewpoints:

- personally
- as a member of a family
- as a citizen of a country
- as a member of the global community.

Both photos show examples of the kinds of difficulties people can face when living in a crowded place. Which of these photos worries you more?

Are you sitting comfortably?

There are probably 20 to 30 people in your classroom. How many more could be added before there were too many? Could you double the number? You might have problems finding seats, or textbooks for the extra people. What would happen if the numbers kept growing?

Now imagine if there were 35 times more people in your classroom – a similar change in world population has occurred over the last 2000 years! This population increase has speeded up in the last 300 years. By 1999 the population was 6 billion. Even though the rate of increase is slowing down, the total population is still rising.

The problems this causes are similar to your classroom explosion. The issues are space, resources and the impact on the environment. Just as in your classroom, people aren't evenly spread. There are unpopular places with few people, and popular places with too many people. The spread of people in an area is called **population distribution**.

A Some of the 430 babies abandoned in a São Paulo children's centre in Brazil. The pressures on poor families are so great that many mothers decide to give up their children in the hope that they will have a better life.

> ### Remember ...
>
> Population is the geographical term for the people who live in a place. It can refer to the people in a village, in a country or even in the whole world.

Key Words!

Population distribution

The way people are spread within an area. The red dots on map **D** show where most people in the world live.

C World population figures

Year	Population (millions)
1750	760
1800	1000
1850	1250
1900	1750
1950	2500
2000	6000

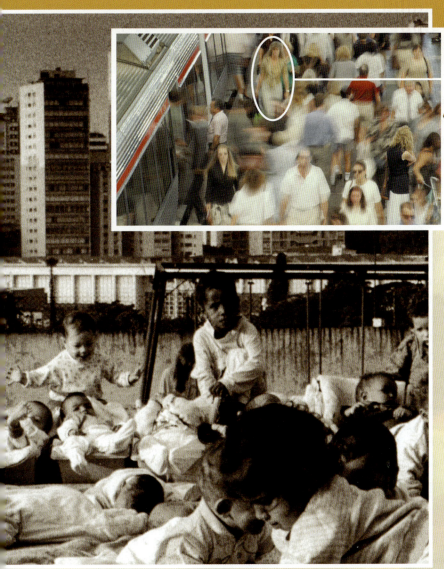

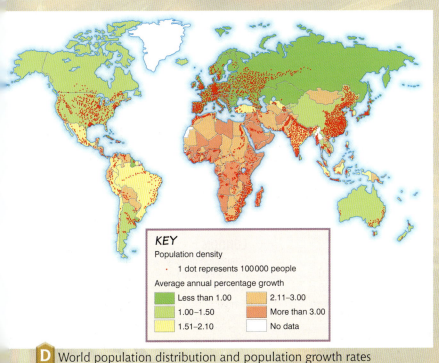

KEY

Population density

· 1 dot represents 100 000 people

Average annual percentage growth

Less than 1.00	2.11–3.00
1.00–1.50	More than 3.00
1.51–2.10	No data

D World population distribution and population growth rates

B Gabriella lives in Madrid. It takes her 3 hours to get to work and back each day, including dropping her child off at nursery. She has decided to have no more children.

1 Write a sentence to explain what 'world population' means.

2 Draw a line graph to show the increase in world population using the figures in table **C**. Make sure the x axis along the bottom goes up to 2030.

3 Read the following statements and choose three as labels to add to your line graph:

Signs of a slowing down of the growth rate

It's suddenly getting very crowded

A few more people are being born than are dying

Population has doubled since 1930

This is the fastest rate of increase

4 Plot how you think the graph will develop between 2000 and 2030.

5 Explain what the graph tells you about the changes in world population. What do you think will happen in the future?

6 Look at map **D** and the map of the world on back cover resource **F**.
  a Name three countries that seem to have a high population density. *Hint*: They will have lots of red dots on map **D**.
  b Name three countries that have a low population density.
  c Describe the pattern of where people live in the world. Try to use words like *many/few*, *north/south*, and *even/uneven*. For example: *In Australia most people live on the south-east coast*.
  d Using map **D**, put the following countries in the order of their population growth. Start with the highest first.
  China Mexico Kenya Spain South Africa
  e Do you think the most populated countries are growing the fastest?

Where do we all live?

The way people are seated in your classroom, or where people stand at break time, is rarely an accident. It is just the same for the distribution of world population. There are many reasons why some places are more popular and are *densely populated* and why some places attract fewer people and are *sparsely populated*.

Total population

All the people who live in one place (e.g. a town or a country).

Population density

The number of people who live in an area of land. It shows how closely people live together.

How many is too many?

If we add up all the people who live in one country, we know the **total population**. But this may not tell us all we need to know. All the people crammed into your classroom would have had plenty of room in the hall. We need to know the space available (**area**) and then the **density** (how many people live in an area of land). Population density is calculated like this:

$$\frac{\text{Total population}}{\text{Area}}$$

For example, the total population of England is 48.5 million people. The area is 130,000 km².

$$\frac{48.5 \text{ million}}{130\,000} = 373.1$$

Therefore the population density of England is 373.1 persons/km².

People are attracted to live in places with 'positive features' that make life easier, such as flat land. These places have a higher population density. People are less attracted to live in places with 'negative features', like mountains where life is difficult. But even where climate and landscape are extreme, humans have the ability to change the natural environment to suit their needs.

GRAMPIAN MOUNTAINS

Population density (persons/km²)	Under 10
Altitude	600–1100 m
Terrain	Steep slopes
Climate in winter (°C)	2–3°C
Soil	Thin sandy soils

Population density in the UK

A

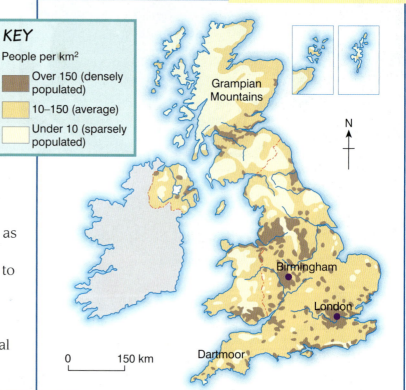

KEY

People per km²

- Over 150 (densely populated)
- 10–150 (average)
- Under 10 (sparsely populated)

Grampian Mountains

N

Birmingham

London

Dartmoor

0   150 km

BIRMINGHAM

Population density (persons/km²)	Over 150
Altitude	100–200 m
Terrain	Gentle slopes
Climate in winter (°C)	4–5°C
Soil	Thick sandy soils

DARTMOOR

Population density (persons/km²)	Under 10
Altitude	200–600 m
Terrain	Quite steep slopes
Climate in winter (°C)	4–5°C
Soil	Thin sandy soils

LONDON

Population density (persons/km²)	Over 150
Altitude	Under 100 m
Terrain	Gentle valley slopes
Climate in winter (°C)	5°C
Soil	Thick river valley alluvium and gravels

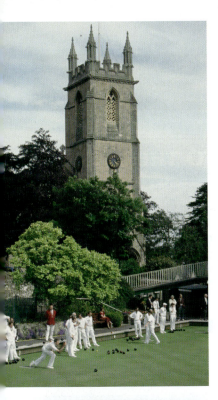

B

Factors affecting population distribution

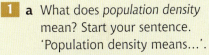

OVER TO YOU

1 a What does *population density* mean? Start your sentence. 'Population density means…'.
b Explain why population density is more useful than the figure for total population. You need to think about numbers of people and the size of the area they live in.

2 Using map **A** and a physical map of the UK in an atlas, explain why each of these areas attracts either more people or less people to live there.

3 For each of the photos in figure **B**:
a Suggest if it is showing positive or negative factors.
b How do those factors make life in that area easy or difficult?
c How would this result in a higher or lower population density?

4 Suggests ways in which areas with negative features could be made more suitable for people to live in. For each suggestion explain why it might be difficult, e.g.

A desert area could be watered but that would be expensive and might take too much water from somewhere else.

How is the population made up?

Population structure tells us how the total population of a country is made up. Population pyramids show population structure. They show how many people there are in each age band. They also show the number of males and females.

Your school population is divided up into year groups, with the number of people in each year changing little every year (see figure **A**). In the real world, population structure changes through time as a country develops.

Working out the reasons for the shape of a country's population pyramid is harder than working out your own school pyramid. However, it tells us much more than just the age of people living there. These population pyramids also show the numbers of **dependents** in a country – that is, the people who are over 60 years of age and those who are under 16 years of age.

The population pyramids for the UK (figure **B**) and Mexico (figure **C**) are very different. The UK pyramid shape is typical of a country that has been growing slowly over a long time. The Mexico pyramid shape is common for countries that have grown a lot recently. Both shapes tell a story.

For example, the UK shape is more even all the way up. In fact it has more over-60s than under-16s, so the average age of the population is rising. We are getting older! The Mexican shape is much wider at the bottom than the top, which means there are far more young people.

PASSPORT · PASSPORT

TO THE WORLD

It is important for countries to know the numbers of their dependents because younger and older people tend to need more support. By studying population pyramids over time governments can predict when new schools and hospitals will need to be built.

A

A school population pyramid

Males

Females

Age

80+
75–79
70–74
65–69
60–64
55–59
50–54
45–49
40–44
35–39
30–34
25–29
20–24
15–19
10–14
5–9
0–4

When do teachers retire ?

Are these the youngest female teachers ?

Could some of these boys be in the 6th form ?

Why are there more girls than boys at this age ?

300   200   100   0   0   100   200   300
Number   Number

1 What does *population structure* mean?

2 a Study figures **B** and **C**. In which country would you be more likely to …
  i be born into a large family?
  ii live until you were 80?
  iii find that your school was overcrowded?
  iv find it easier to get a job?
  b For each answer, say why you think this is so. Use evidence from the figures **B** and **C**.

3 Imagine you work for the Mexican government. You need to predict what the population pyramid for Mexico (figure **C**) will look like in 100 years' time.

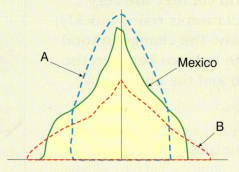

a Do you think it will look more like A or B in the diagram on the left?
b Say why you think these changes will happen, and what it will do to the total population.

Help! Remember that birth rates are starting to fall in many countries that have seen rapid growth. Their population pyramids may become narrower at the base and wider at the top as more people live to a greater age.

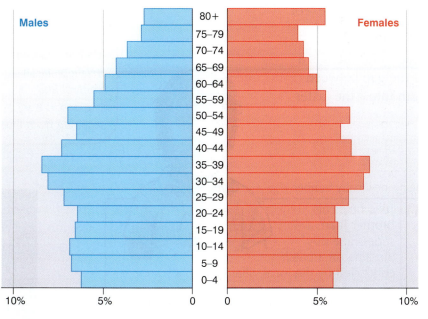

B Population pyramid for the UK, 2000

C Population pyramid for Mexico, 2000

What would happen to the shape of a population pyramid if …?

… more people started having babies?

… new medicine helped people to live longer?

… troops were sent to a major war where many died?

… young men and women went to find jobs abroad in their 20s to 40s?

… a fatal disease with no cure affected the country for 5 years?

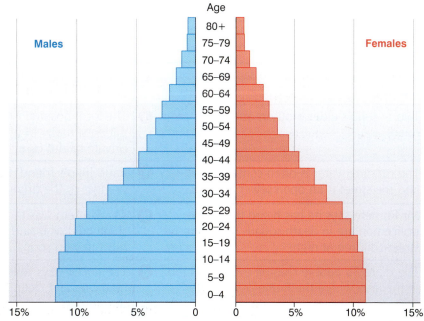

Why is population increasing?

People in Mexico and Spain share the same language and have a similar culture and yet they are very different. In Mexico the population is rising quickly; in Spain it is rising only slowly. The change in total population is the result of the balance between the number of people being born and the number of people who are dying.

The number of people born each year is called the **birth rate**. It is measured out of every 1000 of the country's population. This makes it easy to compare different countries that have different total populations. The **death rate** is the number of people who die in a country in one year, also measured per 1000 people. For example, 10 deaths per 1000 people = 10‰.

When more people are being born than die each year there is a **natural increase** in population. The bigger the gap between these two figures – the birth rate and the death rate – the faster the increase.

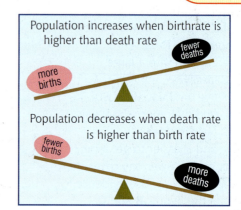

Population increases when birthrate is higher than death rate

more births / fewer deaths

Population decreases when death rate is higher than birth rate

fewer births / more deaths

Three of my seven babies have died... I may yet have another.

My new wife and I hope to have many children – the church is against artificial birth control and besides, it's a blessing from God.

C Mystery – why is Julio Romero unlikely to see his new baby brother

a Julio was born in a shanty town five years ago. He is one of eight children, all living in one room with their parents.	**b** Julio helps his brother Juan, a shoe-shine boy, working on a patch controlled by the local villain.
c There isn't enough food in the house to feed everyone.	**d** Mrs Romero is expecting another child early next year.
e The Romeros wash all their dishes and clothes in an open drain near their shack.	**f** Disease is rife in the shanty town.
g Some street children have disappeared recently.	**h** Shopkeepers and the police believe that the street children are bad for the image of the city.
i Two of Julio's elder brothers and sisters are dead.	**j** The local hospital is overflowing with patients, many of whom cannot afford private health care.
k The running water is often contaminated and the street is an open sewer at times.	**l** Raul, Julio's friend, has asked him to sell oranges to the drivers queuing on the freeway.
m Mr Romero says he has heard that some policemen are in death squads who 'remove' street children at night.	**n** Mrs Romero was threatened by the shoe-shine boss who said Juan owes money and must pay up soon.
o There are 35 people chasing every paid job in the area where the Romeros live.	**p** The doctor says Julio must get proper food, medicine and clean air if his lung condition is to improve.

There's no way I can go to college. I've been working for three years just to help my family cope.

Manolito and I plan to get married as soon as we leave school.

Without more sons I will have no one to help me in my work.

A A Mexican family speaks

I love my two kids but now I think that's enough! I need to get back to my career before others take my place.

B A Spanish family speaks

I would like to live in a trendy apartment in Madrid when I'm older but when I told my dad he just laughed and said 'and what if you and your wife want a family, Mr Moneybags?'

I want to be a doctor when I grow up. I guess I'll be 25 before I qualify, then I'll need to work hard for 10 years before I think of having a family… We are taught that the church says birth control is wrong but I'm not sure my girlfriends agree.

My daughter hopes to become a doctor when she's older. She will need a lot of money to support her… but she won't be supporting my old age! She hopes to travel to the USA to work.

OVER TO YOU

1
 a When the birth rate is greater than the death rate in a country, does the total population increase or decrease?
 b Explain or illustrate your answer.

2
 a What do the following terms mean?

birth rate **death rate**

natural increase

 You can use the Glossary on pages 126–127 to help you.
 b Write a paragraph to explain how they are linked.

3 Read the comments from the families in photos **A** and **B**.
 a Give at least two reasons why total population is rising rapidly in Mexico.
 b Give at least two reasons why total population is rising slowly in Spain.

4 Which country is more likely to experience a drop in total population by 2050 – Mexico or Spain? Explain your answer.

5 Use the statements in table **C** to work out why Julio is unlikely to see his new baby brother. There is no one simple answer and it may be a combination of factors. Copy each statement onto a separate piece of card. Try to sort them into 3–5 categories according to the similarities and links you see between the evidence on the cards.

Key Words!

Doubling time

This is the number of years required for the population of an area to double its size. If a country of 1 million people has a 3% growth rate each year, it will have doubled in size in 23 years.

A matter of life and death?

If we can see patterns in past population changes we might be able to predict future population changes. Britain was the first country in the world to experience the Industrial Revolution. There was rapid population growth during that time.

About 300 years ago the population of Britain began to increase quickly (diagram **A**). Health and medicine improved in Britain, so more children survived. They had larger families of their own and the population grew dramatically. In the 20th century the birth rate finally began to fall as people chose not to have so many children (see diagram **B**).

The changes that Britain went through happened in other countries later, often at a much faster rate. This was because they could learn from the medical and scientific advances made in Britain and in other developed countries.

Many of the poorer countries of the world (less economically developed countries, or **LEDCs**) are represented by diagram **A**. Many of the richer countries (more economically developed countries, or **MEDCs**) are represented by diagram **B**.

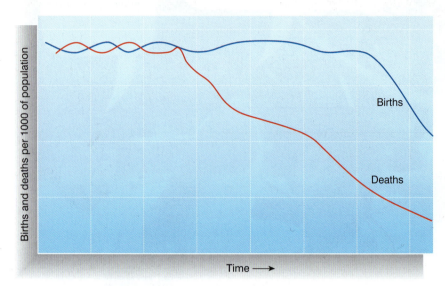

A As a country starts to develop …

D

The University of Life?

UK women who go to university are 50% less likely to have children. The UK government wants 50% of the population to go to university.

Grey Power

Older people are setting up villages in the UK where no one under 45 will be allowed to live. In the USA, there are some counties where you must be 50+ and have $100 000 in the bank to live there. Residents don't see why they should pay for the cost of schooling, childcare and street crime.

B When a country is more developed …

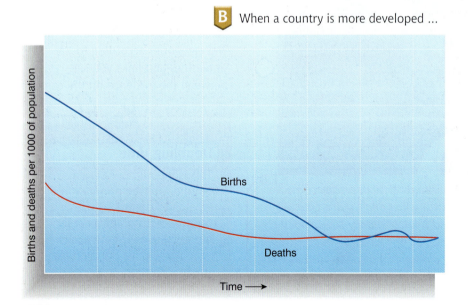

In Britain we have reached a stage where the average couple have 1.7 children.
In other words, the current generation are not replacing themselves for the future.

C Some of the factors that caused population change in the UK

New medicines and hospitals

Improved sewerage and drinking water

Contraception widely available

Better housing

Pensions in old age

Increasing cost of raising children

Education for all

More women going to university

Discovery of contagious diseases

Both parents working

1 a Suggest three reasons why the population of Britain began to increase around 300 years ago.
  b For each reason explain how that factor would affect birth and/or death rates. Use diagrams **A** and **C** to help you.

2 a Suggest three reasons why the rate of population increase in Britain began to slow down in the 20th century.
  b For each reason explain how that factor would affect birth and/or death rates. Use diagrams **B** and **C** to help you.

3 The changes seen in diagrams **A** and **B** took 300 years in the UK. Why might they happen faster in other countries today? Why might this produce more severe problems than Britain faced?

4 Study figure **D**. If countries like Britain have falling birth rates and ageing populations, how might each of the following problems arise? Who might be saying these words? After you have named a likely person or group, suggest a possible solution to their problem.
  a 'I simply cannot get enough workers.'
  b 'Why can't my granddad be treated in hospital?'
  c 'We pay for schools and hospitals by taxing earnings, but there are fewer people to tax.'
  d 'Why should I pay for kids to go to school and vandalise my community? Let their parents pay!'

5 Write a paragraph to support one or both of these statements:

Many rich, developed countries with falling birth rates will have problems supporting their older people in the future.

or

A lot of poorer, less developed countries have so many young people there aren't enough jobs and services to go round.

OVER TO YOU

Migration – where do all the people go?

We know the population of the planet is now more than 6 billion. The rate of increase is slowing, but there are still a lot of extra people each year and only limited areas suitable to live in. At the start of this unit, you thought about your classroom becoming overcrowded. Most of you would have seen moving out of the classroom as a good option. But where to, and why?

Migration is the movement of people to another region or country to work and live. Someone who moves into your region is an **immigrant**. They are an **emigrant** from the region they have left. Most British people are descended from immigrants if we look back in history (as you will see in Unit 6). What makes people take the brave and often dangerous decision to migrate?

Migrants may have many reasons for moving. Some are related to the bad things about the place they wish to leave (**push factors**). Others are a result of good things about the place they would like to move to (**pull factors**). Often their reasons are a combination of both.

1. Look carefully at photo **A**. What is the story behind the picture? What questions would you need to ask to find out the truth behind the image?

   Try making up 10 questions about what is happening in the picture. Think of a range of questions which might begin with *Who? When? Where? What? Why?* – and you could add *How?*

2. What is meant by the terms 'push factor' and 'pull factor'?

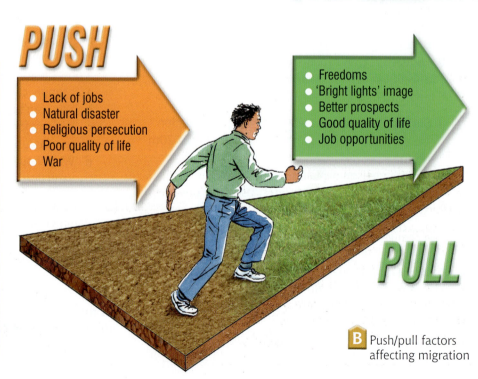

PUSH
- Lack of jobs
- Natural disaster
- Religious persecution
- Poor quality of life
- War

PULL
- Freedoms
- 'Bright lights' image
- Better prospects
- Good quality of life
- Job opportunities

B Push/pull factors affecting migration

A What's the story?

3 **a** Write out the meanings of these key words:

immigrant   **migrant**   **emigrant**

b Explain how all three are linked.

4 Choose **three** of the following statements and say if you think the cause of the migration is a *push* or a *pull*. What evidence did you use to make your decision?

> When the rains failed for the fifth year I had to leave Eritrea.

> There is so much more opportunity for young people in London. I find the North East is dull in comparison.

> I'll work here for two years more then go back to my village in Turkey.

> Under the religious laws in Nigeria I would not be free today so I moved for my freedom.

> The same job back in Mexico would have earned me less than one-third of what I earn in California.

5 Read the text in box **C**. Try to identify two push factors and two pull factors. For each factor say why they contributed to Pedro Paez's decision to move to Spain.

6 Transfer the push and pull factors onto a copy of diagram **B**. How is this diagram likely to be typical for many migrants across the world today? How is it likely to be different?

7 Many geographers predict that migration will increase steadily in the years ahead. Use the following key words to suggest why that might or might not happen:

population growth   **mobility**

scarce resources   **transport**

communications   **ageing population**

What goes around comes around   **C**

Pedro Paez and his family left their home town of La Rioja, in the shadow of the Andes on Argentina's wild western frontier. The economy was collapsing and some of the poorest children were dying of hunger. Pedro now lives 6000 miles away in a small, remote Spanish village. The Paez family were brought from Argentina to help save the village from a decades-long decline in population which threatened its very future. The Paez family has travelled back along the path of the first conquistadores and the generations of Spanish emigrants who followed them to South America. His neighbour, Gilda Mazzio, commented, 'My parents-in-law emigrated to Argentina to flee the poverty here in Spain. Now they wonder whether they should have stayed. But who knows, maybe my children will find themselves forced back to Argentina one day.'

Migration – the salvation of the nation?

One effect of the ageing population in the UK is that there are fewer younger people to join the workforce. Britain badly needs the new input of younger skilled workers. If job vacancies cannot be filled by young Britons entering the job market, then bringing in skilled people from abroad may be the answer. The addition of qualified workers from abroad means that although the UK birth rate is falling, the total population has risen to around 60 million.

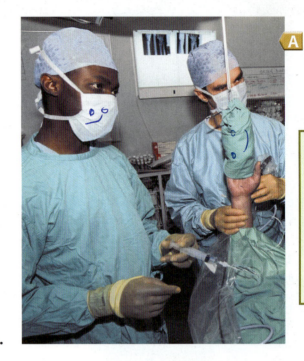

A The health service depends upon the expertise of many immigrants and descendants of immigrants

Selected shortage occupations
Teachers
GPs and consultants
Nurses and midwives
Software engineers
Railway, road and bridge engineers
Veterinary surgeons
Accountants

B Migrant occupations welcomed by the UK government

Navpreet Singh – Not speaking the language was very hard at first and the weather was much colder and wetter than in Uganda. In 1973 our children were young but just of school age. I had to work in the clothing factory to make ends meet.

Diljeet Singh – I used to help my mum out with the phone calls and shopping until she got a bit more up to speed! In 1985 I went to university to study medicine. I began work as a GP in 1991. One of my children started playing for the Warwickshire County Cricket Youth team in 2002. The other wants to be a vet.

Sharanpal Singh – We arrived in England in 1971 after being forced to leave Uganda, like many East African Asians. I was a successful businessman in Kampala but got a job here in Coventry cleaning in the local car factory. It was nine years before I moved onto the production line.

C The Singh family – starting again

Parminder Singh – I found school difficult to get used to and was really pleased to get a chance in my uncle's business in 1983. It was a real eye-opener in terms of hard work. I realised that working in the shop wasn't what I wanted, so I went to evening classes in accounting from 1988 onwards. It took me ages to get all my qualifications part-time, but I finally became a chartered accountant in 1997. I moved to London in 2003 to work in a major firm. There is a chance of working in the USA – I hope!

D Without immigration we would lose...

E 1970 1975 1980 1985 1990 1995 2000 2005

OVER TO YOU

1 **a** Choose two of the photos in **A** and **D**, which show some of the contributions made to life in the UK by immigrant families in the UK.
  b Explain why each might be important to you.

2 The UK government welcomes immigration from some groups of skilled workers. Figure **B** lists some examples.
  a Select two of the occupations shown in figure **B**.
  b How might your life be different if there were not enough migrants to do these jobs?

3 **a** Draw a large timeline like figure **E**.

  b Read the family histories in figure **C**. Then add labels below your timeline to show when the Singh family benefited from moving to Coventry.
  c Mark each benefit for the family alongside the correct date **below** the line and shade it *red*.

4 **a** Read the story in figure **C** again and identify how the Singh family have helped the community in Coventry and the UK.
  b Mark each benefit to the community alongside the correct date **above** the line and shade it *green*.

5 Choose three pieces of evidence from your timeline to help you complete each of the following:
  a 'Immigrants to a new country can find life difficult because ...'
  b 'They often start to contribute quite quickly to the local economy as ...'
  c 'In time, immigrant families become more integrated into society because ...'

6 'What happens next?' Annotate the right-hand side of your timeline **E** to indicate what might happen to any member of the Singh family in the future.

Settlement – why do we live where we live?

What do you know about *settlement*? More than you think. Try listing 10 things you like about the place where you live. Other people in your town would add more attractions to the list, because we all value different things.

The people of Hereford in photo **A** have many reasons for valuing the place where they live. How many of these reasons are absolutely essential to everyday life? How many are just desirable? How many were valuable some 2000 years ago when the first Hereford was being settled?

A settlement can be a single house or, like Mexico City, a place where over 20 million people live. Each one has a **site**, which is the land the settlement is built on. It also has a **situation**, which is how that settlement relates to the surrounding areas. When a settlement is first developing, the factors relating to site may be the most important. Later the situation can affect whether a village grows or dies away.

Hereford has had some form of settlement for around 2000 years but the original attractions of the site and situation may mean little to those who live there today.

Key Words!

Settlement

Settlement is the geographical term for a place where people live.

UK
Hereford

A Why here?

I sold my flat in central London and bought an old farmhouse for less money!

They say the name Hereford is Saxon and means 'ford used by the army'! Well I was in the army and arrived in the 1970s to train with the SAS here.

With my ability to work from home I only need to be in Birmingham three or four days a month.

I came here when my factory moved down from Glasgow in the 1950s. It's so much quieter and with a much lower crime rate than my old city.

I heard it was rated the fourth best city in Britain to live in. There's quite a lot of new housing being built and, as an estate agent, I can tell you it's a popular place.

This work on settlement makes a good introduction to the work on urban growth in *Horizons* Book 2.

Close to navigable river

Rich farmland all around

Roads to five market towns, all within 30 km

On well-drained gravel soil

Lowest bridging point on River Wye (closest bridge to sea)

Ford – crossing for cattle and carts during most of the year

High river bank

Castle mound

Freshwater stream

B Hereford, in 1142

Let's discuss

What do you think you will look for in a village, town or city when you are finding a place to settle? What's more important: low cost, quality of life, how close you are to your job or family? Or is entertainment and level of excitement likely to be the thing that makes up your mind? Try to think of where you would live in your town, in the UK, in Europe or the world. Can you explain your choice?

It feels a bit undiscovered to me. The countryside and pace of life are ideal.

If the kids get bored we just jump on the train to Bristol or Birmingham – we're close enough for a day's shopping.'

OVER TO YOU

1 Diagram **B** shows what Hereford looked like in 1142. Choose two features from the diagram. Explain why these features made it a good **site** for a settlement.

2 Choose two features from diagram **B**. Explain why each of them made Hereford a good **situation** for a settlement.

3 Study the comments of today's inhabitants in photo **A**. Choose three of these and explain if they are related to Hereford's site, situation or to another factor. Arrange your answers in a table like this:

4 a How dependent is Hereford on the advantages of site and situation today?

b What are the new factors that have made Hereford popular in the 21st century? For each one you name, say why it might attract more people to the town.

5 Write *one* of the following:

a An estate agent's advertisement for a new housing estate in Hereford. Think about how it would attract people to the city in the 21st century.

b A poster attracting people to the town of Hereford in 1200.

	Site	Situation	Other
Feature			
Reason			
Feature			
Reason			

raitha

Settlement – is it all about location?

The reason why people started a settlement in the first place often had a lot to do with *site* factors. However, the reason why some settlements grow and others fade away is often much more to do with *situation*.

Hereford is surrounded by smaller towns (map **A**). In the past they needed the county town to provide the **functions** that they were too small to offer. These included law courts, hospitals and administration.

The links between the settlements and landscape are easily seen in front cover resource **A**. They help to explain the way Hereford has grown.

Hereford is on several important routeways: west into Wales, south to the River Severn estuary and Bristol, north towards Shropshire, and east to Worcester and Birmingham. Note how the farmland patterns of the Wye Valley contrast with the uplands of the Welsh hills.

Hereford no longer depends as heavily as it once did on its reputation as a cathedral or market town. Today the attractions of the city are linked to other features.

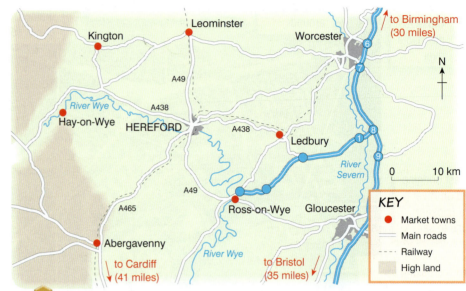

A Where is Hereford situated?

KEY
- ● Market towns
- — Main roads
- --- Railway
- ▒ High land

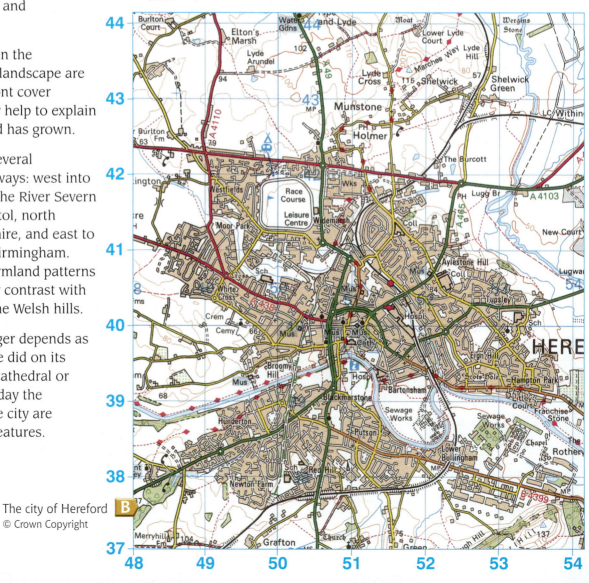

The city of Hereford **B**
© Crown Copyright

1 Study map **B**. Find:

a one grid square with at least two features you can identify from diagram **B** on page 39

b one grid square with no features from that earlier view of Hereford but including some modern housing or buildings.

Answer with four-figure grid references.

2 For the development in **1b**, describe:

a the site and situation of the area (e.g. distance from the river, how close it is to main roads, how far from the middle of Hereford)

b what the height and slope of the land is (e.g. flat, gently sloping, steep)

c how you would get to the following places from your square:
- the railway station
- the cathedral
- the hospital
- the factory at GR 510418 or GR 538379 (whichever is closest).

3 a Why do you think the square in **1b** was chosen as a good place for development?

b Where would you build next if new houses were required? Justify your choice.

4 a Study the maps **A** and **B**, and the comments in figure **C**, which show the reasons why some people live in Hereford today. Try to place the letter from each statement in the correct section of your own larger copy of the Venn diagram **D**. *Remember:* if you think the factor could be in more than one section then you should write it in an overlapping section.

b Choose three of the reasons and explain why they could be located in more than one category.

5 Write a paragraph to explain why you think the shape of Hereford has changed through time.

A My haulage trucks often go to Leominster so I need to cross the new Wye bridge in Hereford.
(GR 507395)

B I sell my sheep and beef cattle at the city's cattle market.
(GR 508403)

C Our hotel benefits from visitors who come to fish for salmon on the River Wye.
(GR 506395)

D The local soils and weather are ideal for growing our cider apples. The area is warmed by the Gulf Stream, so there are no late frosts to damage the blossom.
(GR 541390)

E My plastics firm could have set up anywhere in Britain, but I chose the Rotherwas industrial estate here because the land is flat for building and it's close enough to the main roads.
(GR 524377)

F Tourists love the history of the place! The Mappa Mundi in the cathedral is one of the wonders of the medieval world.
(GR 510397)

G The hospital is a major employer and takes patients from many surrounding towns and villages.
(GR 517402)

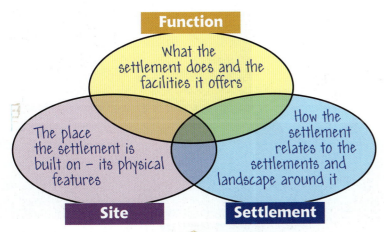

D Hereford – site, situation and function

TO THE WORLD

Many town and country planners have studied Geography to a higher level. The ability to predict changes in population size and distribution in our towns is very useful when deciding when and where to plan new roads, housing and schools.

The Hereford bypass – a decision-making exercise

Are you ready to make a big decision for people in Hereford?

Even though it is a small city, Hereford grew rapidly during the 20th century and is growing still, partly because of migration. New housing means more cars and more journeys. The transport system has not kept up with the times. A new bypass and bridge over the River Wye are proposed to make the best use of the city's situation – but not everyone agrees about the route it should take.

OVER TO YOU

You are President of the Bypass Action Group and need to influence the town council before they vote on the bypass route.

Write a persuasive letter to the town council explaining why the new bypass should take *either* the west *or* the east route. You will need to include map evidence as well as information from the different viewpoints shown in figure **D**. Try to use the following format:

1 Introduction explaining why the new road is needed
2 Why it should follow the west or east route (you decide)
3 Why it shouldn't follow the other route
4 Conclusion

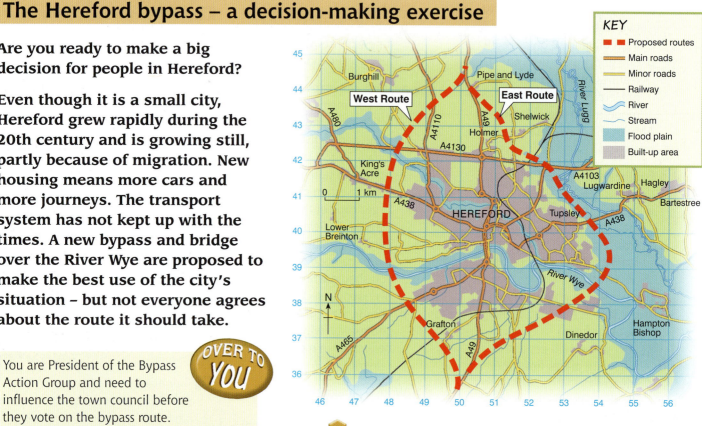

A The possible bypass routes

East Route – **B** the Lugg Meadows (GR 5341)

C West Route – Lower Breinton (GR 4838)

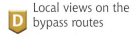
Local views on the bypass routes

What do the local people think?

West Route

FOR

Some of Hereford's major firms are situated on the west and to the north of the city.

There's quite a lot of new housing that needs better access.

It wouldn't be crossing too much flood plain.

AGAINST

On the other hand it does have some high-class housing that some people are keen to keep peaceful.

Some quality farmland would have to be used.

It would ruin the view for the local villages.

East Route

It would be ideal for the industrial estate near Lower Bullingham.

FOR

New housing in this area needs better roads.

It affects less housing overall than the west route.

It would cross a large area of the River Lugg flood plain, which is very prone to flooding.

AGAINST

Some specially protected ancient wildflower meadows would be ruined.

Some valuable farmland and ancient orchards would be spoiled.

By now you have learned some new words in this People unit. Do you know what they mean? One of the best ways to check your understanding is to try to link the facts together.

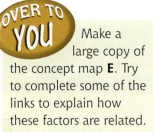 Make a large copy of the concept map **E**. Try to complete some of the links to explain how these factors are related.

Population summary concept map

Falling death rates

Children needed for work and support in old age

Better health care and living conditions

Total population rises rapidly

Birth rates stay quite high

Shortage of food, jobs and housing

Not enough jobs in the countryside

People migrate to find a better quality of life

Cost of living rises

Poverty for many

More houses built

More women are educated and have a career

Contraception is freely available

Large population increases more slowly

Birth rate starts to fall

Cities grow rapidly

3 Rivers

Looking at a river and its valley

Remember ...

Previously in Geography you may have studied rivers. Can you remember how they affect the landscape?

Where are we going?

In this unit you will develop your knowledge and understanding of rivers. You will learn:

- **to select information from photos, diagrams and maps, and to interpret this data**
- **to understand the processes and features of a river valley**
- **to understand the water cycle and the way this affects river systems**
- **why rivers erode, deposit and transport broken rock at different times and in different parts of their courses**
- **how river processes combine to produce landforms.**

You will study one river – the River Earn, in Scotland – in detail. You will see how many features of the Earn, and its valley, are typical of all river valleys. There may be a similar river in your local area.

You can find a map of the valley on front cover resource **B**.

B

A

River Earn

UK

Fantastic Facts

Kelty Burn is about 4 km long from its source to its confluence with Water of May. The Nile in Egypt is the world's longest river at 6690 km.

What is the valley of the Earn like?

C

The photos on these two pages show different parts of the River Earn and its tributaries, the Water of May and the Kelty Burn. The valley of the Earn is in central Scotland, just south of Perth.

Study each of these photos carefully, then complete the 'Over to You' activities.

OVER TO YOU

1 Write a description of the river and its valley in each of the photos. Try to refer to some or all of the following in each photo:

● the width of the stream
● the depth of the stream
● the banks of the stream
● the valley floor
● the sides of the valley
● the speed at which the water is flowing.

Imagine you are standing by the river in each photo. Describe what you might hear and how you might feel in each place.

2 Make sketches of the photos. Then add notes to your sketches to show more detail. You will need sketches of all three photos for your work later in this unit. Either do them by yourself, or share out the tasks in a group.

3 The photos were taken at the following grid references:

● 078142
● 083121
● 087197.

Look at the map, front cover resource **B**. Work out which photo was taken at which reference point.

How do geographers describe rivers?

When you described the photos on pages 44 and 45 you might have used some 'technical terms'. You might have learned some of these terms in Geography before.

If you did, then well done! What were the terms you used?

Now you are going to learn some new key terms. These will help you to understand rivers more clearly, and describe them more accurately. The key terms are divided into three groups:

- terms connected with the water cycle
- terms used to describe the river basin
- terms used to describe how rivers shape the surface to make landforms.

A

Solar radiation	Heat from the sun. This provides the source of energy for the water cycle and for river systems.
Evaporation	Water in the sea, or in river basins, is turned into water vapour (a gas) by solar radiation.
Condensation	When air rises, it cools. The cooling can turn some of the water vapour back into water droplets. These form clouds.
Precipitation	If the water droplets become too heavy they fall, as rain, snow, hail, dew, etc.
Run-off	Some of the precipitation runs off, over the surface. It forms rivers, which run into lakes or the sea.
Throughflow	Some of the precipitation sinks into the surface. Then it runs through the soil, or even through the rock. Throughflow is usually slower than run-off.

B The water cycle

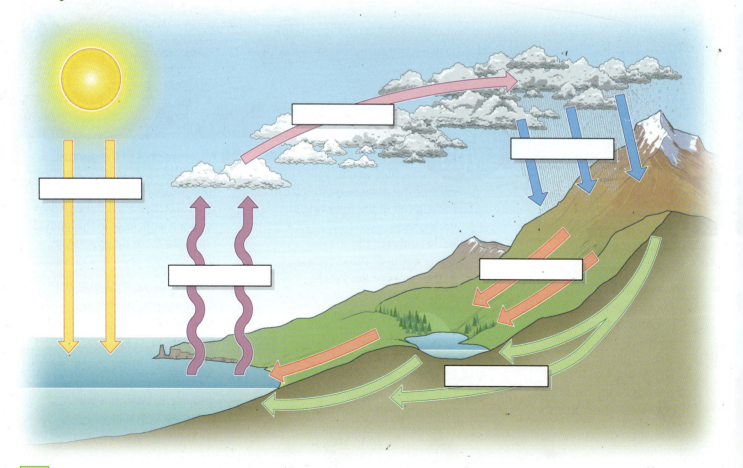

Watershed	An imaginary line through areas of high land. It separates the areas of land that are drained by two neighbouring river systems.
River basin	The whole area of land that is drained by a river and its tributaries.
Source	The place where a river begins to flow.
Tributary	A smaller river that feeds into a larger river.
Confluence	The place where a tributary joins the main river.
Mouth	The point at which a river flows into the sea.
Flood plain	An area of flat land close to a river, which is covered with water when the river floods.

C

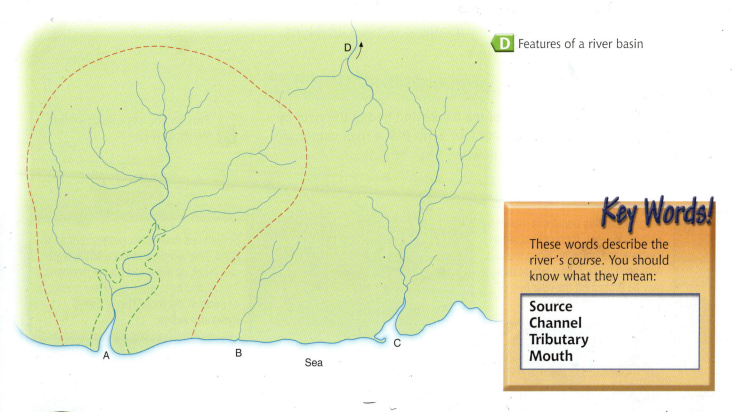

D Features of a river basin

Key Words!

These words describe the river's *course*. You should know what they mean:

> **Source**
> **Channel**
> **Tributary**
> **Mouth**

OVER TO YOU

1 a Label these words on a copy of diagram **B**:
- solar radiation
- evaporation
- condensation
- precipitation
- run-off
- throughflow.

b Write a paragraph to explain how the water cycle works.

2 a On a copy of map **D**, label all the features listed in table **C**. Show them all in the basin of River A.

b Use symbols and shading to represent the features. Take special care when you shade areas. Two of them overlap. You need to make sure that they can both be seen clearly.

c Add a key to your map.

3 Now draw the watershed for River B. Shade the basin. Use a new colour or shade.

4 Draw the part of the watershed between River C and River D that appears on your map. Shade the parts of those two basins which you can see.

5 Finally, go back to your descriptions of the photos on pages 44 and 45. Can you add any of the new words or terms you have learned here to your descriptions of the photos?

How do rivers alter landforms?

What do the words below mean? You might remember some of them from before in Geography.

Weathering   **Erosion**   **Transportation**   **Deposition**

If you are not sure what any of these words mean, look them up in the Glossary on pages 126–127. Make a note of the meaning of each word and try to remember it. You will need to use these words a lot during your Geography course.

Erosion

River erosion is the wearing away of the banks and bed of the river by the power of the river itself. There are four ways that a river can erode. They are all shown on the photo below.

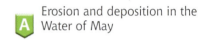 Erosion and deposition in the Water of May

Imagine that this boulder is moved by a strong current. It crashes against the bank and bounces along the bed. With each impact, little bits of rock may be broken off the river bed or bank. This is called **abrasion**.

Sometimes floodwater rushes round this bend. The weight and force of the water can break up the rocks on the riverbank. This works best when there are cracks or joints in the rock. This is called **hydraulic action**.

You cannot see this happening, but river water dissolves some of the chemicals in rocks. The dissolved rock is carried away in **solution**. Then, once some of its material has been dissolved, the whole rock is weakened and can be broken up by other erosion processes.

When the river floods, these pebbles and sand particles are pushed about by a swirling current. They knock together and, with each impact, bits of rock are chipped off and ground up. This is called **attrition**.

Transportation

Once the rock has been eroded it can be **transported** by the river. Transportation also happens in four different ways. They are shown on diagram **B**.

Don't forget that a river can pick up and transport more material when it is flowing faster. If the flow is turbulent this also helps the river move more material.

B Transportation by rivers

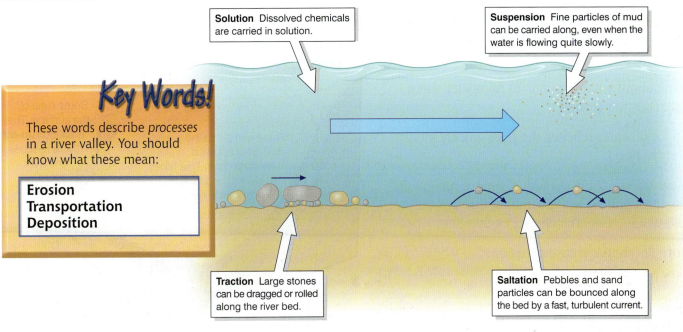

Solution Dissolved chemicals are carried in solution.

Suspension Fine particles of mud can be carried along, even when the water is flowing quite slowly.

Key Words!

These words describe *processes* in a river valley. You should know what these mean:

Erosion
Transportation
Deposition

Traction Large stones can be dragged or rolled along the river bed.

Saltation Pebbles and sand particles can be bounced along the bed by a fast, turbulent current.

Deposition

Rivers have energy in their flow that erodes their valleys. As the volume of water increases, the river gains energy. It will use this to **erode** and **transport** material.

The energy available in a river decreases if:

- the gradient (or slope) of the river is reduced
- the volume of water decreases
- the channel becomes rougher
- water slows down on the inside of a bend
- the channel becomes shallower.

OVER TO YOU

1 Look at photo **A**. Imagine that it starts to rain heavily.
   a What happens to the river's energy level in each of the following stages of a flood?

First: the water covers all the areas of bare gravel on the banks.

↓

Next: the stream fills the whole channel.

↓

At the peak of the flood: the stream spills out of its channel and starts to spread across the field.

↓

Finally: the rain stops and the river quickly returns to normal flow.

b What happens to erosion, transportation and deposition at each stage of the flood? (Don't worry! The farmer made sure that his sheep were safe, long before their field was flooded.)

2 Draw a series of labelled diagrams to illustrate your answer to activity 1.

3 Go back to your annotated sketches of the photos on pages 44–45. Can you add any further notes to your sketches now? Think about erosion, transportation and weathering.

How can people affect a river's flow?

You have seen how the volume and speed of a river's flow can have a big effect on the amount of work (erosion, transportation and deposition) that a river can do. People who live and work in the river basin can also have a big effect on the river's flow. They can speed up or slow down the speed at which water runs off the land into the river. (This is called *run-off*.)

Think about what happens to rainwater when it reaches the ground.

If a lot of water reaches the river quickly it is likely to flood.

Therefore anything that causes more run-off and less throughflow (water running through the soil) will increase the chance of flooding.

More flooding increases erosion.

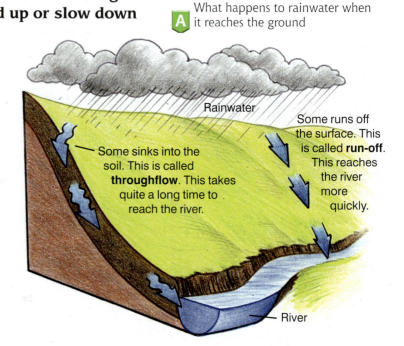

A What happens to rainwater when it reaches the ground

Rainwater

Some sinks into the soil. This is called **throughflow**. This takes quite a long time to reach the river.

Some runs off the surface. This is called **run-off**. This reaches the river more quickly.

River

B

My name is Bob Thomson. I farm most of the land in the drainage basin of Kelty Burn.

People can reduce the amount and speed of run-off by ...

... planting trees and other vegetation, especially on steep slopes.

... leaving unploughed strips round the edges of ploughed fields. This slows down run-off.

People can increase the amount and speed of run-off by ...

... building roads, houses, car parks, etc. because these have surfaces which stop water sinking into the ground.

... cutting down trees and other vegetation. Leaves trap some of the rain and stop it reaching the ground so quickly. Also, plant roots break up the soil and help rainwater sink into the ground.

... keeping too many animals so that they trample the ground and make the surface hard.

C New housing: grid reference 075159 on front cover resource **B**

E Land use: grid reference 088136

D Land use: from grid reference 075148 looking east

OVER TO YOU

1 Look at photo **C**.
  a Why will building this estate have increased run-off?
  b Will this have made the Water of May more or less likely to flood?
  c How might this have affected the people who live by the bridge at 052163 on front cover resource **B**?

2 Look at photo **D**.
  a What evidence can you see – on the far side of the valley – that people have tried to slow down the speed of run-off?
  b What evidence can you see that fast run-off may have been eroding the valley sides?

3 Look at photo **E**.
  a What evidence can you see that the farmer has tried to slow down run-off from the ploughed field?
  b These strips of grass are also called 'beetle banks'. How might they help the ecosystem on farmland? (The ecosystem is the whole community of soil, plants, insects, mammals, birds etc. in a place.)

4 What other evidence can you find on the front cover resource **B** which shows human activity that will:
  ● increase the risk of flooding?
  ● reduce the risk of flooding?
  Be sure that you describe the evidence *and* give a grid reference.

How do rivers deepen and widen their valleys?

Several of the photos of the River Earn have shown that its banks and bed are being eroded. This erosion affects the shape of the valley. The shape of the valley changes as the river flows towards the sea.

Why do these changes happen? They come about because the river erodes both downwards and sideways. However, at some points the river erodes mainly downwards and at other points the erosion is mainly sideways, so the valley shape changes.

Downward erosion (vertical erosion)

Study photo **A**. It shows a hollow on the river bed. The picture was taken from almost the same spot as photo **A** on page 48. Pebbles and sand have been washed into this hollow by the current when the water level in the river was higher. The largest stone in this photo is about 20 cm along its longest axis.

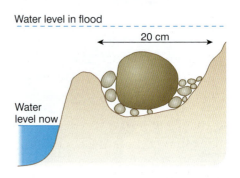

B Cross-section through a pot hole like the one shown in **A**.

Water level in flood

20 cm

Water level now

A A hollow in the river bed of the Water of May

1 Look at photo **A**. After a spell of heavy rainfall the river level rises.
  a What will happen to the speed of the river's flow? (Refer back to page 50 to check this.)
  b What will happen to the pebbles and sand in this hollow as the river flows faster?
  c What will happen to the bottom and sides of the hollow as the pebbles and sand swirl around inside?
  d What effect will it have on the pebbles and sand particles themselves?

Now, imagine this process taking place all over the stream bed. It is helped by the effect of other rock particles being rolled and bounced along the bed. What will happen to the bed of the stream as a whole?

2 The process that you have described in activity 1 is called **pot-holing**. It takes place in many upland rivers where the flow of the water is turbulent and where there are many stones on the river bed.

Write a detailed description of pot-holing. Use these words in your description:

flow   **faster**   **erosion**

attrition   **abrasion**

You might also use some of these words and terms:

turbulent   **deeper**

lowering the bed

V-shaped   **steeper sides**

Look back to pages 48–49 if you need help with these words.

3 Label a sketch of photo **A** to illustrate your answer to activity 2.

Sideways erosion (lateral erosion)

The shape of a river valley is not just affected by downwards erosion. Rivers also erode sideways. The sideways erosion of the channel is caused by hydraulic action and attrition of the banks.

If downward erosion is:	
faster than sideways erosion …	the valley develops a steep-sided, narrow, V-shape.
slower than sideways erosion …	the valley has gentler sides, a broader bottom, and a less steep V-shape.

Rivers near their sources are often quite shallow, because they have not had time to erode very deeply. However, they have quite a clear V-shape.

As they flow further, and come to the edge of the high land, they often become deeper and more V-shaped.

As they near sea level, they cannot erode downwards as much. Their energy goes into eroding sideways. The V-shape opens out and the valley sides become gentler.

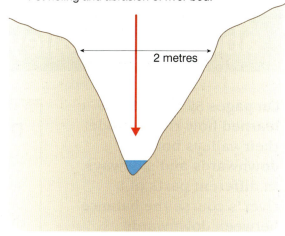

In a V-shaped valley erosion is mainly downwards. Pot-holing and abrasion of river bed.

2 metres

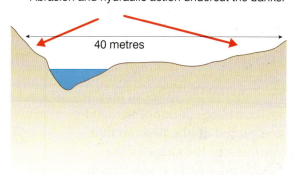

Nearer to sea level, erosion is mainly sideways. Abrasion and hydraulic action undercut the banks.

40 metres

C River valleys change their shape as they near sea level

D Photo **D** shows a tributary of the Water of May.

4 Describe its valley.

5 Explain the main ways that this river is eroding its valley.

6 Try to work out which part of the river is shown here. Is it:
- near its source
- on the edge of the high land
- near to sea level?

7 Make a sketch of this photo. Add notes around your sketch to show how the valley has been eroded.

What can Ordnance Survey maps tell us about river valleys?

On pages 52 and 53 you learned how rivers erode their valleys both downwards and sideways. In different parts of a river's course the balance between downwards erosion and sideways erosion changes. This affects the shape of the whole valley.

Look at diagram **D**. It shows a detailed cross-section through the valley of the Water of May. It is like a slice cut out of the land and placed on the page so that you can see the shape of the landforms clearly. It was drawn from the hilltop at 065140, across the valley, to the hilltop at 087150 (see front cover resource **B**). It clearly shows that, at this point, the valley is a deep, steep-sided, V-shape. There has obviously been a lot of downwards erosion but not as much sideways erosion.

Drawing detailed cross-sections

Cross-sections of other parts of the valley would show different shapes. You can draw your own cross-sections, to see how the shape of the valley changes. The contours on the map show the height of the land, and they also show how steep the land is.

When contours are *close together* the land is *steep*.

When the contours are *spaced well apart* the gradient is *gentler*.

Contours can be used to draw accurate cross-sections.

This is how to draw the cross-section in diagram D:

1 Place a straight-edged piece of paper across the map, between the two grid references.

2 Mark off every point where a contour line crosses the edge of your paper. Record the height of as many of these lines as you can. It will help to remember that:
- Contours are drawn every 10 metres.
- Some contour lines have their height marked on them, in metres.
- Every fifth contour is shown with a thicker brown line. These represent 50 metres, 100 metres, and so on.
- Spot heights are often found at the top of hills and at other important points. These have their exact height written beside them.

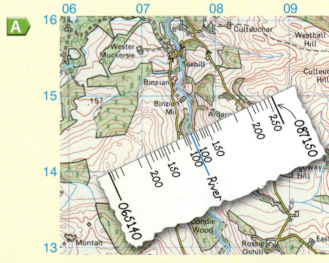
A

E This photo was taken very near to the cross-section

3   Draw a frame for your cross-section. This should be the same length as your cross-section line. Then draw horizontal lines across to show the different heights. (These lines should not be far apart – 1 or 2 mm is an ideal distance.) Add a scale up the side of the framework.

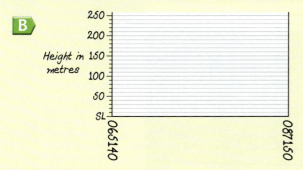

4   Place your rough paper on your cross-section frame, with the ends of the rough paper level with the ends of the frame. Draw a dot on the correct line directly above each contour marked on the rough paper.

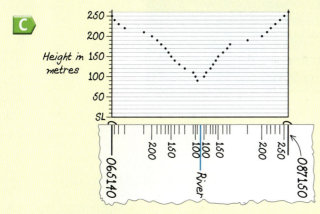

5   Join the points together with a smooth line, to represent the shape of the land. Shade in below the line. Label the main features along the line of cross-section.

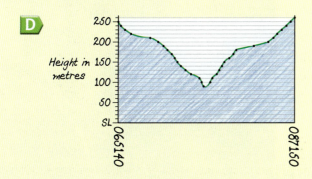

Use the front cover resource **B** for these activities.

1   Draw a cross-section across Kelty Burn from the top of Craigoway Hill 089142, across the valley, to the top of the hill at 091129. (Note that both of these hilltops are just over 240 metres high.)

2   Draw another cross-section across the Earn valley, from the hilltop at 086173, northwards to the hilltop at 075215.

3   Compare the valleys in your three cross-sections. Refer to:
    • the height above sea level
    • the width of the valley
    • the depth of the valley
    • the steepness of the valley sides
    • the general shape of the valley
    • any land use that you can see in the valley, from the OS map.

Help!   Drawing cross-sections from real OS maps is difficult at first. You may want to practise first, using a simpler map. Your teacher may be able to provide a worksheet with a practice map.

What are waterfalls?

Weathering, erosion, transportation and deposition are processes. These processes act on the rocks of an area to produce landforms, such as waterfalls.

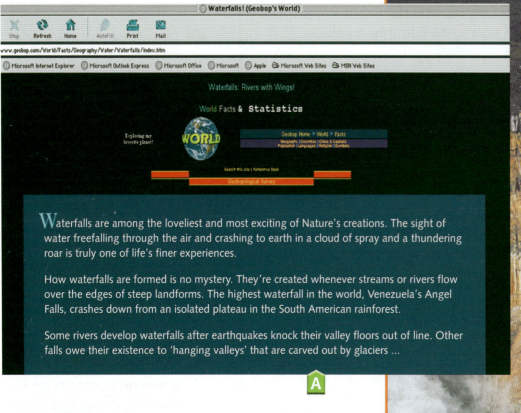

Waterfalls! (Geobop's World)

Stop | Refresh | Home | AutoFill | Print | Mail

www.geobop.com/World/Facts/Geography/Water/Waterfalls/index.htm

Microsoft Internet Explorer | Microsoft Outlook Express | Microsoft Office | Microsoft | Apple | Microsoft Web Sites | MSN Web Sites

Waterfalls: Rivers with Wings!

World Facts & **Statistics**

Exploring my favorite planet!

WORLD

Geobop Home > World > Facts
Geography | Countries | Cities & Capitals
Population | Languages | Religion | Symbols

Search this site | Reference Desk
Geobopological Survey

Waterfalls are among the loveliest and most exciting of Nature's creations. The sight of water freefalling through the air and crashing to earth in a cloud of spray and a thundering roar is truly one of life's finer experiences.

How waterfalls are formed is no mystery. They're created whenever streams or rivers flow over the edges of steep landforms. The highest waterfall in the world, Venezuela's Angel Falls, crashes down from an isolated plateau in the South American rainforest.

Some rivers develop waterfalls after earthquakes knock their valley floors out of line. Other falls owe their existence to 'hanging valleys' that are carved out by glaciers ...

A

WEBLINKS

You will find a link to Geobop's website at
www.nelsonthornes.com/horizons/weblinks

Figure **A** is an extract from a website called Geobop's World. If you visit the site you can learn many strange and wonderful facts about waterfalls, including a list of the world's highest falls, and stories about people who have sailed over the Niagara Falls in barrels! There is lots of good geography, too.

The Angel Falls shown here are the world's highest falls. They are in Canaima National Park, in Venezuela. They are 979 metres high.

Angel Falls

Niagara Falls is probably the most famous waterfall in the world, but it is much lower – only about 55 metres high. However, it is so wide that about 2700 cubic metres of water pass over the Falls every second at peak flow (that is the same as 54 petrol tanker loads of water every second!). Niagara's fame is mainly due to its position, close to the big cities of north-east USA and south-east Canada.

Niagara Falls **C**

Fantastic Facts

Annie Taylor from Bay City, Michigan was the first person to go over Niagara Falls in a barrel ... and she lived!

She was a teacher and claimed to be 43, though she was later proved to be 63 at the time of her exploit. She was strapped into the barrel, lowered into the river, and cut loose. She was pulled out 17 minutes later – dazed, triumphant and famous. When she emerged from the barrel she said, with real feeling, 'No one ought ever to do that again'. In fact, about 10 people have tried since. Most of them were killed.

OVER TO YOU

1 Look carefully at photos **B** and **C**. Working in pairs or in a small group, try to think of words to describe the pictures. Make lists of suitable:
- adjectives
- nouns
- verbs

that match either one picture or both of them.

2 Use your list of words to write a description of each of the waterfalls. You could write your description as:
- an explorer who has just discovered the falls
- a travel agent, trying to sell a holiday to that area
- a holidaymaker (on a trek to the Angel Falls or on a package holiday to Niagara Falls).

Try to write each of your descriptions from a different point of view.

3 a Find photos of other waterfalls. You could cut them from magazines or do a web search. If you do the web search, use the Google search engine. Enter 'Waterfalls' then press the 'Images' tab.

b Write a description under each image that you collect. You could also add arrows to the most important features and write notes with the arrows.

WEBLINKS You will find a link to Google search engine at www.nelsonthornes.com/horizons/weblinks

How do waterfalls form?

On the previous pages you looked at waterfalls and wrote descriptions of them. Now you will go on to see how waterfalls form. Then you will discover how they are eroded and retreat along the course of the stream.

As the web page on page 56 said: 'How waterfalls are formed is no mystery. They're created whenever streams or rivers flow over the edges of steep landforms.'

These steep landforms can be formed where:

- hard and soft rocks are found next to each other – the soft rock is eroded, leaving the hard rock standing much higher
- earth movements push up some parts of the land
- glaciers have eroded their valleys to make them very deep and steep-sided
- sea level has fallen to leave steep cliffs
- sea has eroded the land, again leaving cliffs.

B

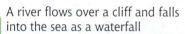
A A river flows over a cliff and falls into the sea as a waterfall

OVER TO YOU

1 On this page there is a list of ways that steep slopes and waterfalls can be formed.

  a Photo/diagram **C** shows High Force waterfall in County Durham. What caused the waterfall to form here?

  b Look at photo **A**. Why is there a waterfall here?
  Use these words and phrases in your answer:

  force of waves   **sea erosion**

  cliff cut back

  c Look at photo **B** and front cover resource **B**. The photo was taken at grid reference 078142. Why is there a waterfall here? Use these words and phrases in your answer:

  highland   **Water of May**   **Kelty Burn**

  larger stream   **vertical erosion**

  powerful   **smaller**   **steep valley side**

As the river falls over the steep drop of the fall it suddenly gains energy. This energy is used to erode the rocks at the bottom of the waterfall. The force and turbulence of the water form a deep pool in the river bed. This is known, for obvious reasons, as a **plunge pool**.

Water swirling around in the plunge pool can erode the rock at the base of the fall. This undercuts the waterfall and forms an **overhang**.

The overhang becomes bigger, until the pressure of water and the weight of the rock makes it collapse. The rocks that crash into the plunge pool are pushed downstream to form a **boulder bar**.

Each time the overhang collapses the waterfall retreats upstream. This forms a deep, steep-sided **gorge** below the waterfall.

2 Choose *either* photo **A** *or* photo **B**. Draw a diagram to show how the waterfall was formed.
Add annotations to your diagram.

3 Turn to page 94. Photo **B** shows a glaciated valley in Norway. There used to be a waterfall here, but the water has been piped. Now, it falls down the pipe and turns a turbine to create electricity.
a Explain why a waterfall formed here.
b Explain why this was a good site for electricity generation.

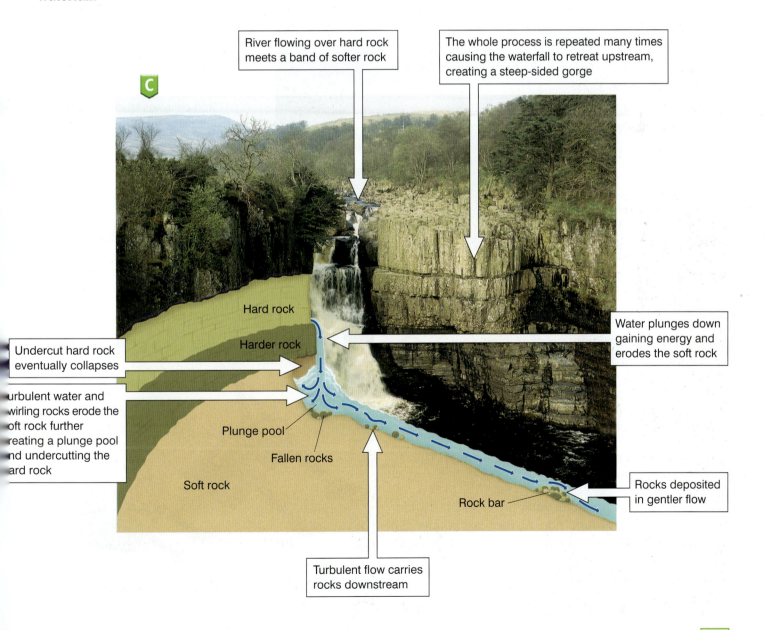

C

River flowing over hard rock meets a band of softer rock

The whole process is repeated many times causing the waterfall to retreat upstream, creating a steep-sided gorge

Hard rock

Harder rock

Undercut hard rock eventually collapses

Turbulent water and swirling rocks erode the soft rock further creating a plunge pool and undercutting the hard rock

Plunge pool

Fallen rocks

Soft rock

Rock bar

Water plunges down gaining energy and erodes the soft rock

Rocks deposited in gentler flow

Turbulent flow carries rocks downstream

59

How does deposition affect landforms?

Look at the course of the River Earn between 049184 (its confluence with Water of May) and the eastern edge of the map on the front cover resource B.

River flood plains are made up of **sediment**, which is fine material that has been carried downstream by the river and then deposited. Thin layers of sediment can build up over the years to form deep deposits. These can give very fertile soil. Photo **A** shows part of the flood plain of the River Earn at grid reference 088197.

OVER TO YOU

1 a Describe the course of the River Earn shown on front cover resource **B**. (Is it straight? Does it bend a little? Does it meander? Are the meanders big? Etc.)'
  b How is the course of the River Earn different from the course of Kelty Burn?'

2 Describe the slope of the land that the River Earn is flowing over. Look at the spot heights and contours close to the river.

3 What evidence is there that this river might have changed its course at some time?

A The flood plain of the River Earn at grid reference 088197

Sediment deposited on a flood plain is usually quite soft. So a river flowing on a flood plain can easily erode the soil and change its course. You can see how this is happening in photo **A**.

This is due to a combination of erosion and deposition by the river. It results from the way the river flows round bends.

On a bend the main force of the water is always concentrated on the outside.

There is less energy on the inside of the bend. The river flows more slowly there.

To illustrate this, remember what it was like last time you went on a fairground ride. As the 'car' you were in was whipped round the bend, did you feel as though your body was being thrown to the outside of the bend and forced against the outside of the car? Something similar happens on a river bend.

B Centrifugal force on a fairground ride

When a river flows round a bend its main current is forced to the outside of the bend. This causes erosion. The current on the inside of the bend is more gentle. It has less energy, so it deposits sediment.

C Water flow on a river bend

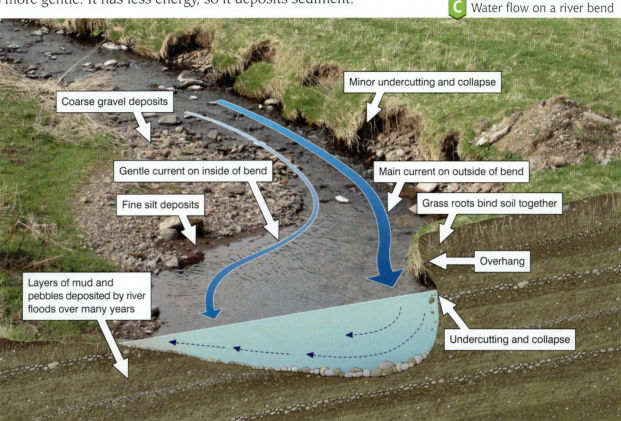

Minor undercutting and collapse

Coarse gravel deposits

Gentle current on inside of bend

Main current on outside of bend

Grass roots bind soil together

Fine silt deposits

Overhang

Layers of mud and pebbles deposited by river floods over many years

Undercutting and collapse

4 Look at photo **D**. It was taken very close to photo **A**. Look for evidence on this photo that erosion and deposition are both taking place.

5 Draw a field sketch of photo **D**. Add labels to your sketch to show *where* erosion and deposition are taking place.

6 Add notes to your sketch to explain *why* erosion and deposition are taking place.

7 Trace one or more of the meanders in the River Earn at:
● 0619
● 120190
● 0518
● 0719.

Add labels to your tracing to show where erosion and deposition will be taking place.

8 Suggest what the stretch of the river that you traced will look like in a few years, if erosion and deposition happen as you expect.

D

Rivers

By now, you will know the river basin of the Earn and its tributaries, the Water of May and Kelty Burn, quite well.

You have learned:

- how water gets into the basin, as part of the water cycle
- how water moves through the basin, the tributaries and the main river
- the processes that are caused by the moving water
- the landforms produced by these processes
- how land use and the movement of water in the river basin interact
- how the features, processes and land use change in different parts of the basin.

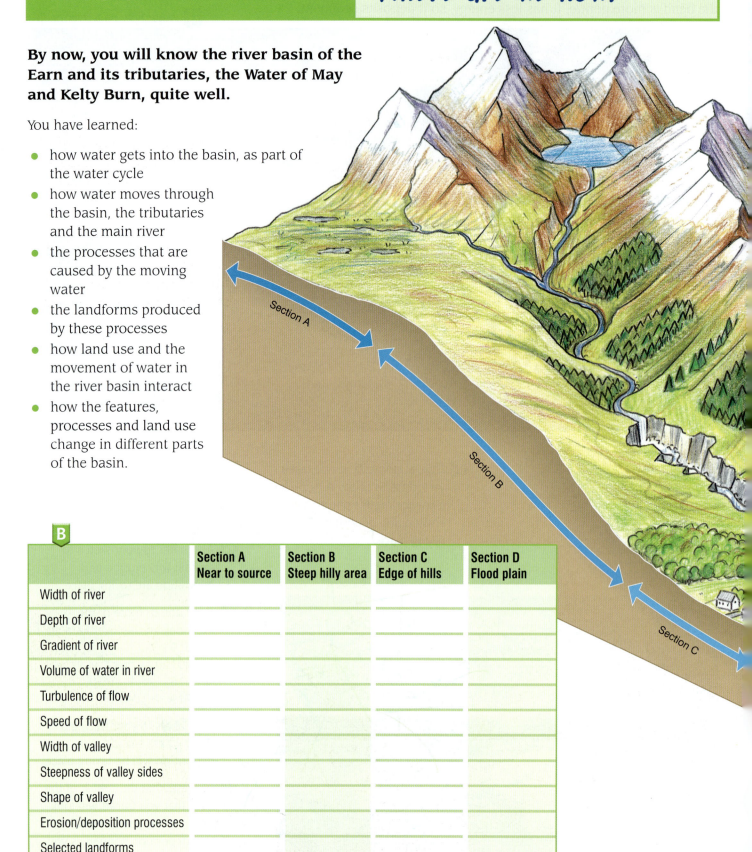

B

	Section A Near to source	Section B Steep hilly area	Section C Edge of hills	Section D Flood plain
Width of river				
Depth of river				
Gradient of river				
Volume of water in river				
Turbulence of flow				
Speed of flow				
Width of valley				
Steepness of valley sides				
Shape of valley				
Erosion/deposition processes				
Selected landforms				
Typical land use				

Much of what you know will be a result of your own enquiry into the basin, using photos and maps. The knowledge and understanding that you have gained from this enquiry can now be used to make some general statements about rivers and their valleys.

As your final piece of work in this unit you are going to produce a summary sheet to include some or all of these general statements about river basins.

OVER TO YOU

Study the river basin in diagram **A**.

1 With a partner, discuss the changes in the river and its valley as it runs from the high land to the sea.

2 Complete a copy of table **B** to describe those changes.

3 Choose two, three or even four of the lines of your table. Explain how the changes that you have described are inter-linked. For instance, you could explain the links between:
- river width, depth and volume of water
- gradient, volume, turbulence and speed of flow
- speed of flow, erosion and deposition processes and selected landforms.

A

Section D

4 Flooding

How do people respond to flooding?

Where are we going?

People need to understand the causes and effects of flooding if they are to manage the problems that they create.

In this unit you will learn about:

- what happens to water when it reaches the ground
- the causes of flooding
- how individuals and communities respond to flooding
- how the effects of flooding in the United Kingdom are different from those in Bangladesh.

Remember ...

In Unit 3 you investigated river landscapes. Rivers are very useful to people. As you discovered in Unit 2, many settlements all over the world have grown around rivers. This can cause problems when too much water gets into rivers and they flood.

B

A

C

Fantastic Facts

Five million people in England and Wales are now at risk from flooding every year.

15 cm of fast-flowing water will knock you off your feet, 10 cm of water will ruin your carpet – and 60 cm of water will float your car!

E

D

Key Words!

Start to create a list of key words and terms to do with flooding. You can start with:

flood

~~cause~~

effect

Use a dictionary or the Glossary on pages 126–127 to find out what they mean.

Look carefully at all these flood photos. They tell a story about flooding and the impact it has on people's lives.

Discuss with a partner what the images show you about flooding.

1 For each photo, list three things that it tells you about flooding. Compare your list with that of a partner.

2 Which floods do you think are in the UK and which are in Bangladesh? Give reasons for each of your decisions.

3 List different ways that people in the photos have responded to flooding.

4 Do the photos show the causes or effects of flooding?

5 Most of the images show dramatic and negative images of flooding, but it does sometimes have positive effects. Do any of these photos show positive effects?

F

What are the causes of flooding?

Remember ...

Look back at Unit 3 Rivers. Remind yourself about the water cycle, how the water gets to the ground, drainage basins and flood plains. This is a useful starting point if you are going to understand the causes of flooding.

Much of the world's flooding is the result of rivers having too much water in their channels. Water overflows the river banks and spreads onto the surrounding flood plains. Flooding can also occur in coastal regions as a result of storms and high winds churning up the sea, creating huge surge waves.

River floods are often the result of heavy rain, but they can also be caused by melting snow. Not all drainage basins react in the same way to a period of rainfall. In some drainage basins rivers rise very rapidly after a storm, causing major floods.

1 Relief
Where a slope is steep, water will flow quickly downhill towards a river. There is little time for it to soak into the ground.

4 Rainfall
A *sudden burst of heavy rain* can cause a flash flood.

A very long period of rainfall can also be a problem. The soil and underlying rock become saturated (filled with water), so that water can only flow over the surface and straight into rivers.

Snowfall can also be a problem. When temperatures rise and the snow melts, large volumes of meltwater are suddenly released into rivers.

2 Rock
Permeable rocks have cracks or pore spaces in them which allow water to pass through them. *Impermeable rocks* do not allow water through them. There is less flooding in areas of permeable rocks because rainwater can pass through them quickly and is stored underground, rather than flowing across the land quickly into river channels.

3 Soils
Sandy soils are made up of grains of sand with spaces or pores in between that water can move through. This type of soil soaks up water very quickly.

A The five main factors that control the way rainwater flows into a river channel

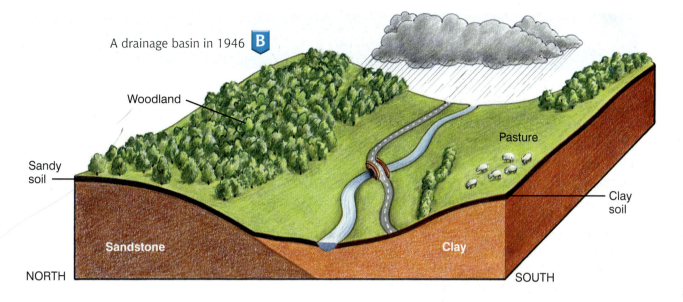

A drainage basin in 1946 **B**

Woodland

Pasture

Sandy soil

Clay soil

Sandstone

Clay

NORTH

SOUTH

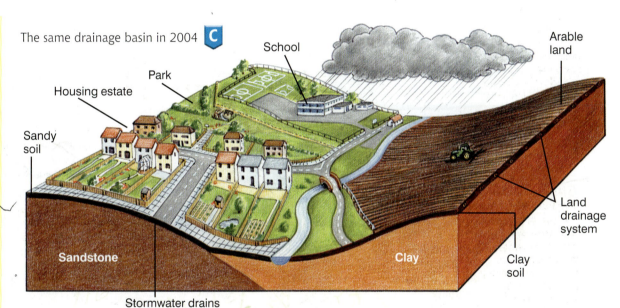

The same drainage basin in 2004 **C**

School

Park

Arable land

Housing estate

Sandy soil

Land drainage system

Clay soil

Sandstone

Clay

Stormwater drains

5 Land use

Plants in a drainage basin store rainfall in their leaves before it is evaporated back into the atmosphere. *Thick forests* can store as much as 30% of a rainstorm, but *crops* only capture 15%, as they are planted in rows with bare soil in between.

The amount of rainfall stored by plants also varies with the *seasons*. In winter, when plants lose their leaves, they store less water. In arable farming areas, ploughed fields intercept no water at all.

Towns and cities increase the risk of flooding, as water cannot soak into concrete and tarmac. Roofs, gutters and drains channel rainwater into underground channels, which often flow straight into rivers.

3 Soils

Clay soils have much smaller pore spaces, so water is slower to pass through. This leads to more run-off into rivers.

1 What is flooding? Start your first sentence 'Flooding is...'

2 Describe five factors that increase the risk of flooding.

TO THE WORLD

Hydrology is the science of the properties of the Earth's water, especially its movement across the land. A hydrologist conducts investigations to measure rates and amounts of surface run-off, in order to predict flooding.

3 Look at diagram **B**.
a Describe the spread of soil and rocks in the area.
b Explain which side of the drainage basin is more likely to flood.

4 Compare diagrams **B** and **C**.
a How has the drainage basin changed over 50 years?
b Explain which side of the drainage basin is more likely to flood in 2004.
c List the different ways in which people have increased the possibility of flooding occurring in the drainage basin.

OVER TO YOU

What caused the York 2000 flood?

The floods that struck England and Wales in autumn 2000 were among the worst ever experienced. York was not the only place to be flooded, though. Autumn 2000 was one of the wettest on record. This caused the most dramatic, widespread and prolonged floods seen for at least half a century.

All rivers in the north-east of England were affected, and some rose to record levels. The peak level of the River Ouse at York early on Saturday 4 November was 25 mm higher than the previous highest level recorded in 1625. A total of 212 properties in York were flooded, roads were closed, and the floods caused damage estimated at £4 million.

Flooding has occurred in York for centuries. The city has grown on the banks of the River Ouse – as you know from your investigation of York in Unit 1 of this book. In 1263, 1316 and 1564, the settlement was swamped by floodwater. More recently, serious flooding occurred in 1947, 1978, 1982, 1991 and 1995.

Flooding along the River Ouse at York is caused by a number of physical and human factors (map **A**).

- The catchment area of the River Ouse north of York covers an area of 3000 square kilometres. The larger the size of the tributaries and the more tributaries there are, the quicker the water will flow into the main river – and this increases the likelihood of floods.

The causes of flooding in the River Ouse drainage basin north of York

- The flooding was the result of the wettest autumn since records began in 1766. After prolonged rain, around 250 mm of rain then fell over a two-week period between 26 October and 8 November 2000. Drainage basins were already fully saturated, and could not hold any more water, so it ran straight into the rivers.

- York is sited at the confluence (place where rivers meet) of the River Ouse and the River Foss, which also increases the risk of flooding.

KEY

Land over 100 metres

- - - Catchment boundary

0   20 km

PENNINES *YORKSHIRE DALES* *NORTH YORK MOORS* *VALE OF YORK*

Northallerton

Thirsk

Swale *Ure*

Ripon

Rye

Nidd

Harrogate

Foss

Ouse

York

Wharfe

Denwent

- The tributaries of the Ouse begin in the Yorkshire Dales and the North York Moors, where the land is steep, so water flows quickly into rivers.

- The removal of peat from the moors, and forest from slopes, has encouraged water to reach the rivers more quickly.

- Changes in farming methods on the flood plains allow water to drain more quickly into rivers.

- The growth of York and surrounding towns and villages, and the building of new roads, cover land with concrete and tarmac. These are impermeable and so speed up run-off into the rivers.

B

C

Estate agents warned that about 450 York properties hit by flooding could lose half their sale value, if they could be sold at all.

'Once the water starts to come in there's no stopping it. It pours across the floors lifting carpets and pushing open doors as it makes its way through the entire downstairs of the house. And it's not clear spring or even river water. It's filthy, smelly water that comes up from the drains and sewage system. It looks and smells horrible; when the water is gone it leaves behind a brown sludgy deposit over everything it touches.'

OVER TO YOU

1 a Use map **A** to name the three main tributaries of the River Ouse, which join it north of York.
   b Which tributary joins the River Ouse at York?

2 Why do tributaries make flooding worse?

3 a Read the information provided with map **A**.
   b Make your own copy of the table below. Add a title: 'Causes of the York flood in 2000'.

Physical geography causes	Human geography causes

   c Write each cause shown on map **A** in the correct column of your table.
   d What do you think was the main cause of the flood?

4 Photos **B** and **C** show the King's Arms public house in 2003, and during the floods in 2000. This building is a popular landmark in York. It is located at grid reference 603517. Find this on the back cover resource **E**. The photos were taken from the nearby bridge.
   a In which direction was the camera pointing when the photos were taken?
   b What class of road crosses the nearby bridge?
   c Use the people standing outside the King's Arms on photo **B** as a scale to estimate how much higher the level of the river was in November 2000, shown in photo **C**.

5 a Read the two quotes below photos **B** and **C**, which are from a York newspaper. Explain why:
   ● a flooded home is unsafe for many weeks after the water has gone

   ● the effect of a flood may last for years.
   b Imagine that you wrote the quote below photo **C**. Describe how you would feel about the flood and the damage it has caused to your home.

6 Use the internet to find your own images of the York flood.
   a Log on and conduct an image search. Type 'York flood pictures 2000' into the search box and investigate the sites that the engine comes up with.
   b Select the two best images that you find on websites. Copy and paste them into your DTP software.
   c Use the DTP tools to label the effects of flooding shown in each image.
   d Add a title to each image. Try to locate each one on the back cover resource **E**. Include a six-figure grid reference in the title for each image.
   e Print out your images.

WEBLINKS You will find a link to Google search engine at www.nelsonthornes.com/horizons/weblinks

What were the effects of the York 2000 flood?

OVER TO YOU

1 Describe the effects of flooding in the area of York shown in photo **A**.

2 Land area **B** in photo **A** has not been built on. Why do you think this is so?

3 Compare photo **A** with the OS map of York – inside back cover resource **E**.

  a In which direction was the camera pointing when the photo was taken?

  b Eleven features are marked on photo **A** with letters. Find these places on the OS map. Then complete a copy of this table (right).

4 Go to the Multimap website.

  a Enter 'York' in the place name box and find the same area shown in photo **A**, at a scale of 1:25 000. Select 'Aerial photo view' on the website.

  b Print out the aerial view and label on it the same features shown in photo **A**.

  c Compare the two aerial photos and draw onto your printout all the areas that were flooded in November 2000.

Feature	Name of feature	Six-figure grid reference
River feature A		
Land area B		
Bridge C		
Building D		
Building E		
Land use F		
Building G		
Road H		
Village I		
Building J		
What crosses bridge K?		

WEBLINKS You will find a link to Multimap at
www.nelsonthornes.com/horizons/weblinks

A North-west York, looking towards Clifton Bridge which crosses the River Ouse: November 2000

Key events in the York flood 2000

5 What does this mean? →

Wednesday 25 October A *Flood Watch* is issued by the Environment Agency for the whole of the Vale of York.

6 What does this mean? →

Sunday 29 October Initial warnings from the Environment Agency about rising floodwaters – a *Flood Warning* is issued for Kings Staith, grid reference 603517.

7 a What does this mean? →

Tuesday 31 October 12.21 pm: First *Severe Flood Warning* received in York, where Huntington Road runs alongside the River Foss, 6052.

b Look at the OS map of York. Identify where you think the A19 would be flooded. Give the six-figure grid reference and → explain your chosen location.

A19 at Fulford is closed.

c i Find the village of Naburn on the map: is it north, south, east or west of York?

ii Give the four-figure grid reference for the village. →

iii Use map evidence to explain why you think it was cut off.

The village of Naburn is cut off completely. A *Severe Flood Warning* had been issued for the village on **29 October**.

8 Give a grid reference for where you think the A19 is flooded. →

Friday 3 November The A19 is closed at Rawcliffe, between the stream next to the Ouse and the lake.

Severe Flood Warnings are issued by 22.15. Much of the city is put on Severe Flood Alert. Predictions show the river level is likely to top the flood defences at Leeman Road, grid reference 597519. The army pile up sandbags here to increase the height of the defences.

C The army sandbagging on Leeman Road

B

Flood warning codes

The flood warning system consists of the following codes with the following messages.

 Flooding possible. Be aware! Be prepared! Watch out!

 Flooding expected. Affecting homes, businesses and main roads. Act now!

 Severe flooding expected. Imminent danger to life and property. Act now!

 All clear. Check all is safe to return. Seek advice.

Crisis Point

Friday 3 November During the evening, engineers pumping water from the River Foss into the Ouse, at the Foss Barrier pumping station, report that they are experiencing difficulties as there has been a massive increase in river flow along the Foss. The police and the Environment Agency investigate this development and discover that the Ouse has begun to overflow into the River Foss at Tower Street, grid reference 604515.

9 a What problems will this cause ↑ in grid square 6051?

b What part of the city is this?

The army sandbaggers must leave Leeman Road immediately and block the overflow. Unfortunately, the quickest route along the B class road is blocked by floodwater.

10 a Use back cover resource map ↑ **E** to work out the best route for the army sandbaggers to take.

b Write down directions from Leeman Road to Tower Street. Include the numbers of the roads the army lorries should follow and the direction they should travel on each road.

c To help them reach their destination quickly, the police closed roads and a bridge to traffic. Identify which you think they were, and give their grid references.

The Ouse peaked at 3 am on **Saturday 4 November** at 5.4 metres, just 5 cm below the top of the flood defences. The level of the river slowly began to fall, by Sunday at a rate of 2.5 cm an hour. The Environment Agency issued the *All Clear* on Tuesday 7 November.

11 What does this mean? ↑

How well is York protected from flooding?

The 2000 flood was the worst flood experienced in York, and yet only 212 properties were flood damaged, and although some roads were affected, the city centre remained open for business throughout the disaster.

This was due to the system of flood defences developed over a period of years by the Environment Agency. Without these defences over 5000 properties would have been flooded, costing at least £10 million. The flood schemes in the city are shown on map **A**.

The Foss Barrier

As you discovered on pages 70 and 71, one of the major flood hazards facing York occurs at the confluence of the Ouse and Foss rivers. A rapid increase in the volume of water in the Ouse can force the water in the Foss back, causing it to flood surrounding properties. This was a major factor in the 1947, 1978 and 1982 floods in York.

The Foss Barrier was developed to isolate the Foss and the Ouse, at a time of flood, with a movable barrier. A pumping station was also constructed, allowing the normal flow of water from the Foss to the Ouse, but stopping water from the Ouse backing up into the Foss. A flood wall was also constructed to help separate the two rivers.

The whole scheme was constructed in 1987 for £3.34 million. During November 2000 the barrier worked continually, well beyond its design limits, pumping 23 million gallons of water each hour into the Ouse.

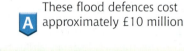
These flood defences cost approximately £10 million

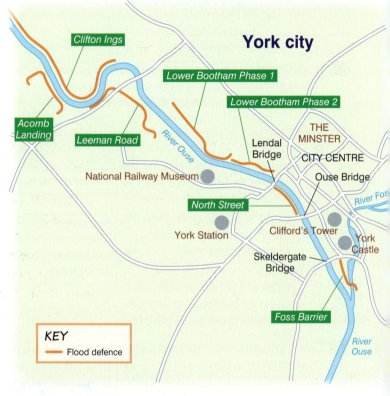

York city

Clifton Ings
Lower Bootham Phase 1
Lower Bootham Phase 2
Acomb Landing
Leeman Road
River Ouse
THE MINSTER
Lendal Bridge
CITY CENTRE
National Railway Museum
Ouse Bridge
River Foss
North Street
York Station
Clifford's Tower
York Castle
Skeldergate Bridge
Foss Barrier
River Ouse

KEY
— Flood defence

Barrier

To the Ouse

River Foss

The Foss Barrier **B**

F Sluice gates on the Ings

North Street

This part of York city centre includes many shops, housing and commercial properties. In 1992 and 1993 a series of flood gates and walls were constructed to protect the area.

Lower Bootham

Floods have regularly caused problems in this residential area. The flood of 1982 caused £1.2 million of damage to 134 properties. In 1983 a scheme was developed, involving the construction of a 650 metre earthen flood bank, together with a 280 metre reinforced concrete wall. Each house has a steel gate and wall near the front door for added protection. Similar defences protect residential areas at Leeman Road and Lower Ebor Street.

Acomb Landing

This is the location of the water treatment works that provides fresh drinking water to York. It is vital to the city that this site remains free from flood contamination. After the 1982 flood, a reinforced wall was added to the existing embankments.

C Flood wall on North Street during the November 2000 flood. Its height was increased with sandbags.

Flood gates for each house

Flood wall

D Earlsborough Terrace, Bootham

Wall protecting waterworks at Acomb

E Acomb Landing during the November 2000 floods

Clifton Ings

This is the flooded area in photo **A** on page 70. It is a natural flood plain which can store 2.3 million cubic metres of water, lowering the peak flood level in York by 150 mm. In 1982, at a cost of £1.25 million, flood banks were raised and new embankments constructed to increase water storage. Sluice gates were also built to let water in and out of the Ings.

OVER TO YOU

1 Compare map **A** with the back cover resource **E** of York.
   a Match the three named bridges shown on map **A** with their six-figure grid references:

   Lendal Bridge   **Ouse Bridge**

   Skeldergate Bridge   **599519**

   604513   **602517**

   b Give the six-figure grid reference for each of the following:
      i   the water treatment works at Acomb Landing
      ii the Foss Barrier
      iii North Street.

2 a What are the advantages and disadvantages of the flood protection schemes in York? Choose at least one scheme, e.g. the Foss Barrier, North Street, etc.
   b Write a paragraph to summarise your findings about the effectiveness of York's flood defences.

3 Now you have read this page (especially the section headed Clifton Ings) go back to activity 2 on page 70. Try to write an even better answer to that question now.

Environment Agency: can it cope with floods?

The *Environment Agency* is the main government agency for coping with flooding in England and Wales. It is responsible for building flood defences and looking after them. It is also responsible for warning people if a flood is likely to happen. People can prepare for flooding by knowing about flood warnings and flood protection. This is why the Environment Agency runs a Flood Awareness Campaign every year.

Although flooding cannot be prevented, there is much that a developed country like the UK can do to limit the worst effects of flooding.

Fantastic Facts

Around 5 million people, in 2 million properties, live in flood risk areas in England and Wales.

1.9 million homes and 185 000 businesses are at risk of flooding in England and Wales – property, land and assets to the value of £214 billion.

A How the Environment Agency helps us to cope with floods

Identifies areas of England and Wales that are most at risk from flooding

Recommends the building of flood defences where they are most needed

Continually monitors rainfall and river levels using datalogging equipment to judge when a river is likely to flood

ENVIRONMENT AGENCY

'Flooding – you can't prevent it, but you can prepare for it.'

Issues flood warnings to the public through the media

Alerts and works with emergency services such as the police, fire brigade and army to provide help for those who are at risk

Raises public awareness of how to prepare for and cope with flooding

Links to... This investigation of the Environment Agency links to your Citizenship studies where you are required to study the work of government agencies.

B Environment Agency advertisement – part of a flood awareness campaign

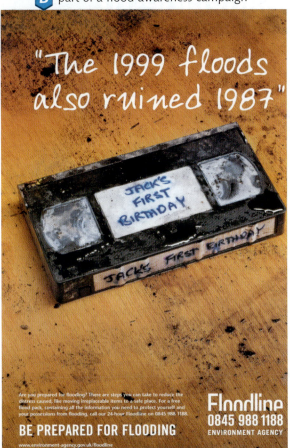

"The 1999 floods also ruined 1987"

JACK'S FIRST BIRTHDAY

Are you prepared for flooding? There are steps you can take to reduce the distress caused, like moving irreplaceable items to a safe place. For a free flood pack, containing all the information you need to protect yourself and your possessions from flooding, call our 24-hour Floodline on 0845 988 1188.

BE PREPARED FOR FLOODING

www.environment-agency.gov.uk/floodline

Floodline
0845 988 1188
ENVIRONMENT AGENCY

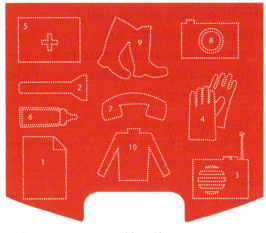

MAKE A FLOOD KIT
KEEP IT SAFE AND EASY TO REACH

Include:
1 important personal documents
2 a torch
3 a wind-up or battery-powered radio
4 rubber gloves
5 a first aid kit

6 baby essentials
7 important phone numbers
8 a disposable camera
If you receive a flood warning, add
9 wellington boots
10 waterproof clothing

Other items you may wish to include are a mobile phone, food and water

Floodline
0845 988 1188
ENVIRONMENT AGENCY

C An Environment Agency poster

1 What is the Environment Agency?

2 'Flooding – you can't prevent it, but you can prepare for it.' What is meant by the quote shown in diagram **A**?

3 Use diagram **A** to describe three ways that the Environment Agency can reduce the risk of flooding.

4 Look carefully at the advertisement **B**.
a What is its purpose?
b Explain the statement: 'The 1999 floods also ruined 1987'.
c Do you think that the advert is effective in raising awareness?
d Why does the Environment Agency need to spend money on adverts like this?

5 Look carefully at the poster **C**. List the items in the Flood Kit and explain why each item is needed.

6 a Investigate the Floodline section of the Environment Agency website.
b How does the Agency use the internet to inform people about flooding?
c Enter your postcode in the box provided on the Floodline homepage, in the 'What's in your backyard?' section.
d A map of your local area will download. Select Flood Warning areas from the 'Show layers' box. Wait for the map to download. Is your local area a flood risk? Print out your flood risk map.

7 In a small group, develop your own flood awareness campaign.
a Choose three or four key messages and explain how you will tell people about them.
b You could use ICT to help you:
• Evaluate the current awareness campaign on the Environment Agency Floodline website. Conduct searches about flood awareness using Google.
• Present your campaign as a six-panel leaflet using DTP software, or as a PowerPoint presentation.

OVER TO YOU

WEBLINKS **You will find links to Google and the Environment Agency at** www.nelsonthornes.com/horizons/weblinks

What causes flooding in Bangladesh?

Flooding in Bangladesh happens every year, and the Bangladeshi people are usually well prepared. Problems can occur when the floods are much greater than usual, or happen with little or no warning.

Over the last ten years or so, Bangladesh has suffered a number of very severe floods. These floods were partly caused by the country's physical and human geography, and partly by the country's human geography – see photo *A*.

Key Words!

Cyclone

An area of low pressure in the Indian Ocean and the western Pacific Ocean, which causes strong winds and heavy rain. The term 'hurricane' is used in other parts of the world.

Monsoon

A weather season in which very heavy rainfall affects the regions that border the Indian Ocean, in South East Asia.

Fantastic Facts

- Bangladesh is a country in South East Asia.
- It is one of the poorest countries in the world.
- 80% of the population live in rural areas.
- Only 30% of men and 19% of women are literate.
- 60% of children suffer from malnourishment.
- In Bangladesh flooding can be caused by rivers or by tropical cyclones on the coast.

OVER TO YOU

1 Compare photo **A** with back cover resource **D**. Name the following on photo **A**:
- countries A to D
- rivers E and F
- physical features G and H
- cities I and J.

2 a Read the labels on photo **A** outlining the causes of flooding in Bangladesh.
  b Make your own copy of the table below. Add a title: 'Causes of the flooding in Bangladesh'.
  c Write each cause shown on photo **A** in the correct column of your table.

Now decide how important each cause is. Lightly shade the boxes on your table to show:
Very important causes – *red*
Important causes – *orange*
Other causes – *pale yellow*

Physical geography causes	Human geography causes

3 Write an explanation of the physical causes of Bangladesh's floods. You should include sections on:
- the relief of the land
- the monsoon
- cyclones.

4 At this point in your study, do you think that the river floods are the most important cause of the floods in Bangladesh?

5 Explain how each of the following has made the flooding worse in Bangladesh:
  a human activity in Nepal
  b human activity in Bangladesh.

6 Photo **A** is a satellite image taken in August 2002. It is a true- and false-colour image taken aboard NASA's Terra spacecraft. In the false-colour image, land is green or orange, and water is dark blue to black.

In late summer 2002, heavy monsoon rains led to massive flooding in eastern India, Nepal and Bangladesh, killing over 500 people and leaving millions homeless. This image shows the extent of this flooding.
  a Look carefully at photo **A** and back cover resource **D**. Which of the two major rivers which flow through Bangladesh appears to be flooding ?
  b Why do the colours change from green in the northern areas shown on the image ?

7 The satellite image **A** was downloaded from NASA's Visible Earth website.
  a Go to this website and see if you can search the site to download your own copy of this or a similar image showing flooding in Bangladesh.
  b Copy and paste your image into your Desktop Publishing software, and use the software tools to label the features in activity 1.

The population of Nepal is increasing. Trees have been cleared in the foothills of the Himalayas to make way for farming and housing. This has increased the speed at which water flows into the rivers. As a result, erosion and the amount of material carried by the rivers have increased.

Bangladesh is one of the most densely populated countries in the world and its population is increasing. More and more of the land is farmed and covered by buildings.

Bangladesh is a low, flat country – 80% of it is less than 6 metres above sea level, so it is easily flooded.

Bangladesh is the combined delta of three major rivers: the Brahmaputra, the Ganges and the Meghna. The drainage basins of these rivers cover an area over 1.6 million square kilometres – 11 times larger than the country itself. The sources of the rivers are in the Himalayas.

The period of heavy rains coincides with the year's highest temperatures. High rainfall in the Himalayas combines with melting snow and glaciers to swell the rivers.

The floods bring an important benefit to Bangladesh. They deposit silt on the farmland, and this helps to keep it fertile. Farmers depend on some flooding to grow their rice crop.

The whole of Bangladesh has been formed from silt deposited by rivers from the Himalayas over millions of years.

Tropical storms, or cyclones, blow from the south bringing strong winds and heavy rain. The winds cause big waves, leading to coastal flooding. As much as 50 mm of rainfall can fall in one hour, and 200 mm can fall in a day – but such heavy rainfall does not usually fall over a large area.

The monsoon rains blow north from the sea. The rain is often torrential. In 1998 these rains were heavier than ususal.

The shape of the Bay of Bengal channels the winds as they blow towards the coast.

Bangladesh has a monsoon climate. This means that most places receive between 1800 and 2600 mm of rainfall a year, but over 80% of it falls from May to September.

As the rivers get near to their mouth they deposit silt, which blocks the main river channels and raises the river bed. The increase in river erosion in the Himalayas means that the rivers are carrying more silt, making this even worse.

WEBLINKS You will find other satellite images on NASA's Visible Earth website at www.nelsonthornes.com/horizons/weblinks

Dhaka Weekly

22 September 1998

The worst and longest flood in our history!

Bangladesh is in the grip of the worst and longest floods in its history. They began when monsoon rains triggered flash floods in the north in June. Torrential rains in July brought on further floods throughout the south-east.

According to the latest government statistics, about 70% of the country and two-thirds of the capital Dhaka have been flooded. More than 2000 people have died from drowning, snakebites and disease. New areas are affected daily, and between 30 and 40 million people are living in temporary shelter. A large number of cattle have died and most of the autumn rice crop has already been destroyed. This is expected to result in food shortages in a few months from now which, aid workers say, could be life-threatening for millions of people.

Aid worker Julian Francis surveyed some of the remote districts by seaplane. He said: 'It was difficult to know where rivers ran, the expanse of water was so dramatic. Except for a few buildings in one or two towns I could not see any dwelling place which was not affected by the worst floods this century. The water has been on the ground for more than a month in many areas.'

News correspondent, Francis Harrison, says that the country can cope with some seasonal flooding, but the longer the water remains on the ground the more hardship it will cause. It is the duration of the current flood rather than the depth of the waters – which is not unusually great – that is causing the problems. Lack of sanitation and drinking water mean that disease is the main killer.

Hospitals throughout the country report 175 000 cases of serious diarrhoea – a disease that can be fatal, particularly to young children. At least 140 people have died already after eating rotten food or drinking dirty water.

In Dhaka, the country's capital, the stinking, stagnant water is polluted with sewage, waste and dead animals. One relief worker described conditions in Dhaka: 'On some rooftops in the flooded eastern suburbs of the capital parents tie up their small children with ropes or chains so that they do not slip into the floodwater and drown. This happens, especially when the child's father and mother are both away seeking relief goods, leaving their babies in the care of their younger brothers and sisters.'

The dignity and the courage of the people is inspiring. People have taken to fishing in a big way, since the one thing the floods have done is to increase the supply of fish. In fact, there is such a large increase in fishing that fish prices have fallen by a third. People have dismantled their houses for use in building rafts. Plastic sheeting, commonly used as a building material, has become the most valuable item that people possess.

Flood survival support

The Bangladeshi Foreign Minister appealed for international aid for millions of people left homeless or destitute. These are the initial priorities to help people:

1 Food distribution

Through the initial appeal, the aim is to provide 100 000 families with 30 kg rice and 5 kg lentils or with chira and gur (compressed rice and molasses). The distribution areas will be selected based on the flood situation at the time of distribution.

2 Vegetable seed distribution

With most of the seed beds in the affected areas destroyed, the need for crop and vegetable seeds is enormous. It is intended to supply vegetable seeds to 100 000 families to supplement their family diet and income in the post-flood situation.

3 Medical services

One hundred mobile teams will work for a period of 30 days in the affected areas, focusing on lung infections, and waterborne stomach and skin diseases. The teams will also monitor the nutritional status of vulnerable groups and provide special supplementary food.

4 Water containers

Because of the contamination of tube wells and because people have to carry clean water to their homes, 50 000 families will be provided with plastic water containers.

5 Clothing

Due to the harmful effects of water and humidity, an urgent need for garments for the most affected women has been identified and 100 000 sarees will be distributed.

---

1 Describe the effects of the 1998 flood on Bangladesh.

2 List the different causes of death of people in the flood.

3 Why did the length of time that Bangladesh was flooded create problems for people?

4 Describe things that people did to try to survive the flood.

5 Explain the following:
a The flooded area was unsafe for many weeks afterwards.
b The effect of the flood may last for years.

6 Imagine that you were one of the survivors of the flood. Describe how you would feel about the flood and the damage it has caused to your home.

7 Read the section above about 'Flood survival support'. Explain the choice of the five initial priorities to help people.

8 Use the internet to find your own images of the Bangladesh flood.
a Conduct an image search using the Google search engine. Type 'Bangladesh flood 1998' into the search box. Select the image tab and investigate the sites that the engine comes up with.
b Select the best images you find on websites, and copy and paste them into PowerPoint slides.
c Imagine you are a picture editor for a newspaper. Add captions to your chosen images in your PowerPoint presentation to tell the story of the flood.
d Justify your choice of images.
e Print out your images.

OVER TO YOU

PASSPORT · PASSPORT · PASSPORT · TO THE WORLD

Unfortunately, every year there are natural disasters somewhere around the world. Many charities and aid agencies conduct worldwide appeals to help people cope with these disasters. Your school could conduct a campaign to help people cope with such a disaster, perhaps working with a charity.

WEBLINKS You will find a link to the Google search engine at www.nelsonthornes.com/horizons/weblinks

How can Bangladesh cope with floods?

The following extract is based on an article published by an international group of engineers and geographers who had studied the problems of Bangladesh.

A

... most politicians, journalists and engineers see floods as the major hazard in Bangladesh. Local farmers think river erosion is a much bigger problem than monsoon floods. Floods are part of the daily life of farmers. During abnormal floods life is hard, but after the water goes down the land is again available. Over generations people have developed ways of dealing with floods. Erosion, however, is a silent disaster, which takes away the life-support systems of whole families.

Based on these findings, widespread, traditional thinking about flood management in Bangladesh must be revised. Cyclones are certainly the most critical and damaging hazards in Bangladesh. In combating monsoon floods the most important measure is the preservation of *beels* (lakes) and swamps for the storage of surplus water. Large embankments that keep water in the rivers sometimes make the floods worse. They may stop small floods, but they can also keep valuable water off the rice fields.

In a large flood they make the river too full and too fast. Then, the flow can erode the land very seriously. What is more, if the barriers break, floodwater can rush suddenly across the land, eroding it and sweeping away homes, animals, and even people.

The article below is taken from a news report during monsoon floods in Bangladesh in 2000.

B

My driver told me that this flood was not unusual, and that the water had come more than a metre higher in 1998. Even so, it had flooded most of the houses to a depth of around 50 cm. Most of the women and children, along with their animals, were crowded onto mounds of earth around the edges of the village. These had been built for just such emergencies. Meanwhile, the men were still at work on the land. Most were repairing the low banks around their fields, getting them ready to keep enough water, when the floods retreat, for growing the next crop of rice.

One village had not been flooded. It was protected by a large bank which kept the flood water safely away to the west. The local men were busy maintaining this bank, but then we heard a murmuring from the other, flooded side. Their bank was being attacked by their neighbours, who lived nearer to the river.

They were poorer people who had been forced to farm land that flooded more easily. They could see that the new bank, built to protect one piece of land, was stopping water from draining off their land. The attackers tried to break a hole in the bank to drain their land. The police soon arrived and arrested the leaders of the attackers. The rest soon left – to go back to protect their families and property. Because they were so short of land there was no mound for them to keep dry on. They just had to sit on piles of their possessions.

D A refuge mound

A flood shelter **E**

C

Other suggestions to reduce the problems of flooding in Bangladesh include:

- building 'refuge mounds' that rise a metre or so above the level of the land (photo D)
- building concrete shelters on tall legs, about 4 metres above the level of the land (photo E)
- buying a radio for the village to listen to weather forecasts
- developing systems of signalling with flags, to show the wind strength predicted by the weather forecasts
- burying emergency supplies of food about half a metre below the soil surface
- storing emergency food supplies on platforms about 1.5 metres above the ground
- buying a boat
- tying down the roof of the house – like using guy ropes on a tent
- improving roads, to make it easier to evacuate the area
- tying up the animals, to stop them running away in panic
- buying large metal tanks to store fresh water
- building a wall from mud, sticks and straw, to keep out floodwater.

OVER TO YOU

1 Bangladesh has to plan to avoid two types of flood risk.
  a What are these two types of flood risk?
  b Which type is the more serious threat to people?

2 Look at photo **E**.
  a Describe how these shelters will helps save lives in a flood.
  b Imagine you are a flood warden. What equipment would you store in the shelter in case of a flood?

3 Work in groups and decide which of the solutions in **C** would be:
  a useful for poor farmers living on the banks of the Ganges, but too far inland to be seriously affected by cyclones
  b useful for poor farmers living on the coast, but not near to a river that floods regularly.

  Give reasons for your choices.
  Try to explain why you chose some – and also why you rejected others.

4 **a** Why does article **A** say that it is important to conserve *beels* and swamps?
  b How will this help:
    - reduce flooding
    - give more irrigation water for a longer period of rice growing?

5 Imagine that you lived in the area described in the news report **B**. Work in pairs. Take the following roles:

  A a farmer from the 'river side' of the embankment, who wants it destroyed

  B a farmer from the 'dry side' who wants it maintained.

  Using photos **D** and **E** and list **C** to help you:
  a List as many points as you can in favour of your preferred solution.
  b Then try to think of a 'compromise solution' which you could both accept.

How do floods in the UK and Bangladesh compare?

Both York and Bangladesh suffer from a high flood risk. You can now think about how floods in the two areas are similar and how they are different. Look back through this unit and think about the causes and the effects of flooding.

OVER TO YOU

1 The Brown family live in York. In 2000 their house was flooded. Graph **A** shows the flow of the river that caused the crisis.

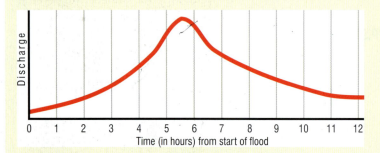

A Flood hydrograph of the River Ouse

Draw a copy of the graph **A** and annotate it to show when each of the Brown family reactions in diagram **C** probably took place.

2 How might things be different for a family in Bangladesh when their home is threatened by flooding? List ten things that might happen to a family in Bangladesh. Add these as labels to another copy of the graph.

3 On page 69 you drew a table showing the causes of floods in York. On page 76 you drew a similar table for Bangladesh. Look back to those two tables.

Draw a Venn diagram, like diagram **B**, to show:
a causes that only affect York
b causes that only affect Bangladesh
c causes that are common to the two places.

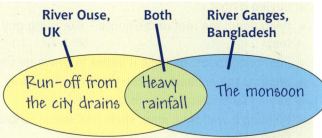

River Ouse, UK   Both   River Ganges, Bangladesh

Run-off from the city drains   Heavy rainfall   The monsoon

B Venn diagram: the causes of floods

4 Which causes might be fairly easy to solve, and which will be more difficult? Shade them on your diagram in different colours.

5 On page 70 you wrote about the effects of the York flood, and on page 82 you wrote about the effects of the Bangladesh flood. Now draw another Venn diagram, this time to help you compare the effects of flooding in Bangladesh and the UK

6 Use the information in your Venn diagram to write a comparison of flooding in the UK and Bangladesh. You could begin your writing like this:

Flooding in the United Kingdom and Bangladesh had a large number of effects. In many ways the two floods had very different effects. These differences included ......

There were also several similarities in the two floods. These were ......

In conclusion, I think the floods in .... had a greater effect than in .... because...................

Ten things that happened to the Brown family during the flood C

1 John calls the insurance man

Mary cleans the carpet 2

3 Rachel cancels her trip home

Mr Brown checks the current state of the flood on the Environment Agency's floodline website

5

4 Will fills the sandbags

6 The local shop is running out of mops

The radio forecasts heavy rain 10

7

Rachel phones home worried

8 The insurance assessor arrives

9 The firemen pump water out of the street

5 Work

My world of work!

Where are we going?

In this unit you will develop your knowledge and understanding of the different types of work that people do. You will learn:

- how to divide people's jobs into different types of employment: primary, secondary and tertiary

- about farming (a type of primary activity) and how farmers have to work closely with their environment

- about the manufacture of sports goods (a secondary activity) and the differences between mass production and specialised production

- about work in call centres (a tertiary activity), and the way that developments in ICT have opened up a whole new area of employment.

What is work?

Key Words!

Primary workers

produce raw materials from the land. This work includes farming, fishing, forestry and mining.

Secondary workers

work in manufacturing industry. They take the raw materials and make them into finished products.

Tertiary workers

do not produce 'things'. They provide services for people.

Geographers divide 'work' and 'workers' into three groups. These are primary, secondary and tertiary.

This is a very basic classification idea in geography. You could apply it to jobs you have seen in previous units, such as Flooding and People.

To illustrate some of these ideas you will be asked to think about people you meet every day and the work they do... but first think about the workers whom I met one Saturday...

Saturday

In the morning I went to the gym. I met Lorna, a trainer, who showed me one of the new machines and started to work out a new programme for me.

I bought a paper then had lunch at a local café. The waiter brought me sea-food salad, a pizza and a half bottle of Italian wine.

In the afternoon I went into town. I bought a map, a CD and a shirt.

That evening I went to a concert. Nicola took my ticket. I went home on the Metro.

1 Look at my day.

Make a list of the people I have met, who have done work for me. Put these people into three different groups of:

a primary employment

b secondary employment, or manufacturing

c tertiary employment, or services.

2 The three groups in your answer to activity 1 were probably not very even. So go back and try to find some of the jobs that supported those workers.

For instance, the diary might also have said...

> The sea-food salad was made up of fish, lettuce and tomatoes with oil and vinegar dressing. I had some bread with it too, made of flour that had been baked by a baker and transported to the shop by a driver ...

Try to find at least six more people who have done primary work for me, and at least six who have done secondary work.

3 Make a list of the people who have done work for you today – or think back to the weekend if you prefer. Add in the other workers who supported the people who worked for you 'face to face'.

Make a display to illustrate this title:

My world of work (primary, secondary and tertiary)

You could use a word-processing package, with clipart or photos to provide illustrations.

What work do we do in the UK?

On page 85 you were asked to see what types of worker you came into contact with most: primary, secondary or tertiary. Did it turn out to be tertiary or service employment? It was in my case.

In fact, most of the jobs in the UK are in the service sector. The proportion of jobs in services has been growing steadily over the last 40 years and more, as table **A** shows.

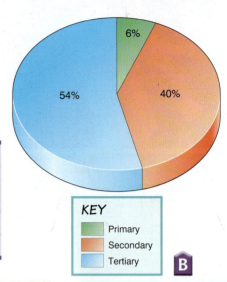

	Primary	Secondary	Tertiary
1964	6	40	54
1979	7	37	56
1999	4	27	69
2002	4	26	70

A Percentage of all UK jobs in each sector of employment, 1964–2002

KEY
- Primary
- Secondary
- Tertiary

B

1. Illustrate the figures from table **A** by drawing four graphs – one for each year. Use bar charts or pie charts. If you use pie charts the first one has been done for you – see diagram **B**.

2. Study your pie charts and describe the changes in:
   - primary employment
   - secondary employment
   - tertiary employment
   in the UK between 1964 and 2002.

3. Study the pairs of pictures on these pages – C and D, E and F, G and H. Pick out some of the reasons shown for the changes in the number of people employed in the primary and the manufacturing sectors.

4. The workforce in agriculture in the UK has fallen very rapidly during the last 50 years. Use the figures in table **I** to draw a line graph showing this fall.

Year	Number of workers	%
1955	1 500 000	5.1
1984	698 000	2.8
1992	637 000	2.4
2002	550 000	1.9

I UK workers in agriculture, 1955–2002

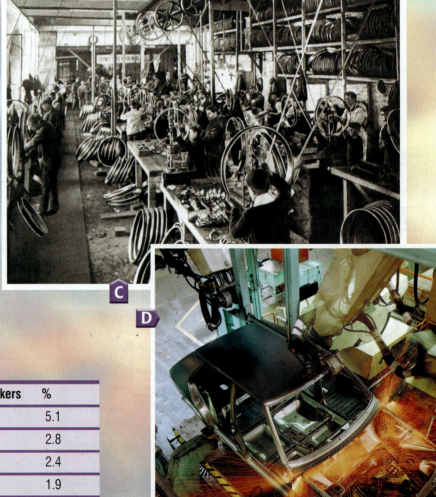

C

D

E

F

H Imported cars ready to be sent all round the UK

G The 'I'm Backing Britain' campaign in the 1960s tried to increase exports and cut imports

I'M BACKING BRITAIN

Fantastic Facts

In the mid-20th century, Sunderland produced more than a quarter of the UK's total tonnage of ships. It was probably the most important shipbuilding town in the world. Sunderland's last shipyard closed in 1988.

How has farming changed?

On page 86 you saw how the number of farmers in the UK is falling. Now you are going to look at changes in farming in more detail. You will learn about the Aireys' farm in Lancashire. It is called Black Moss Farm.

Black Moss is a dairy farm. It produces milk. Some of this is sold to customers as fresh milk. Some goes to a cheese factory. If you drink milk or eat cheese you might have consumed a product which started as a raw material at Black Moss!

A The location of Black Moss Farm

B Wayne and the big tractor

My grandad said that farmers will soon evolve without legs, because we do so much of the work on quad bikes and such. He didn't realise that life on a farm moves at a much quicker pace now than in his day.

I can't remember a time when I didn't help out on the farm. I probably started to do useful jobs with the cows when I was about 11. Once I was 13 and could drive a tractor, I became really committed.

D Adam goes to bring the cows in for milking

C Herd size over time

Number of milking cattle on Black Moss Farm

THINK ... again!

People who live in cities often think of farmers as simple people who are a bit out of touch with the modern world. Is this true?

Look at these pages for evidence of farmers and
(a) education
(b) mechanisation and
(c) investment in their business.

A history of the Aireys and
Black Moss Farm **E**

1 a Where is Black Moss Farm?
 b Name the four members of
   the Airey family.
 c What is the main product from
   the farm?

2 Use a large copy of graph **C** to
 draw a living graph of Black
 Moss Farm.
 a Label your graph with facts
   about the Airey family, e.g. in
   1998 write:

   Adam starts to work on
   the farm.

 b Use a different colour of pen –
   or a tracing paper overlay – to
   write comments about the EU
   and CAP, e.g. in 2005 write:

   EU subsidies for milk
   will be stopped.

 c Use a third colour – or another
   overlay – to write comments
   about investment in Black
   Moss, e.g. in 1995 write:

   Extra land rented from
   a neighbour.

 d Finally add a section for other
   factors that you think are
   important.

3 Study your finished graph. Try to
 find five links between different
 labels on your graph. Write them
 out as in the example below:

   1973

   UK joins EU. Good
   prices guaranteed to
   dairy farmers.

   Black Moss increases
   size of herd.

4 Copy and complete the
 following sentences (right) to
 summarise changes on Black
 Moss Farm. Fill in the blanks
 using the word bank.

Year	
1965	Bill Airey (John's dad) moved to Black Moss and rented the land from a big estate. He kept 44 cows for milk. There were three full-time workers and two part-timers.
1973	The UK joined the European Union (EU). The Common Agricultural Policy (CAP) guaranteed good prices to dairy farmers.
1981	The CAP was becoming too expensive. Quotas were introduced to limit the amount of milk that farmers could produce.
1989	Bill retired. John had worked on the farm since he left school. Now he and his wife Emmie took charge.
1992	Wayne (their son) left school. He went to agricultural college part-time for six years but also worked on the farm. He has stayed at Black Moss since then.
1993	The estate owners sold the land. With the aid of a large bank loan the Aireys bought their farm. They modernised, and increased the size of their cattle herd.
1994	BSE ('mad cow disease') was spreading. This is a cattle disease that can spread to humans. It never hit Black Moss, but it caused big worries for the Aireys.
1995	Black Moss Farm is only 136 hectares. The Aireys started to rent 20 ha of extra land from a neighbour, so that they could keep more cattle.
1998	Adam (the younger son) left school. He has worked on the farm since then – with some study at college and a year out travelling to Australia. Now there are five workers on the farm: four of the family and a cowman.
2000	The EU will phase out subsidies and quotas on milk production by 2005. This will probably benefit large, efficient farms.
2001	The foot and mouth crisis led to the deaths of tens of thousands of cows. Again, Black Moss escaped infection – but many dairy farmers gave up farming.
2002	Things were difficult on the farm. Profits were very low. John and Emmie thought about selling up and leaving farming. The family talked things over. Both boys want to stay farming here... so they decided to plan for the future and hope for the best. They invested in a brand-new, state-of-the-art computerised milking parlour.
2003	The new milking parlour is working and the Aireys have increased the milking herd to 175. They are planning to build up to 200 milkers. They will do this by keeping more of the calves that are born on the farm. At present they sell a lot of them as soon as they are born.

Black Moss Farm has become more efficient because it has _____ cattle now than it did in 1965. In 1965 it had _____ cows and by 2005 it will have _____ . The family only use _____ extra worker to look after these cattle. Output per worker has _____ . One reason for the improved efficiency has been _____ . They have invested in _____ , _____ _____ and a state-of-the-art _____ _____ . All this saves time and _____ _____ .

mechanisation   **more**   **milking parlour**   **quad bikes**

tractors   **increased**   **wage costs**   **1**   **44**   **200**

Why is primary employment decreasing?

How have the Aireys been able to increase the size of their herd of cows with only a small increase in labour? The main reason is 'mechanisation'. Until the 20th century milking had always been done by hand. Now machines do most of the work.

Early milking machines had tubes that fitted onto the cow's udder. A vacuum was created and the milk was drawn from the cow and passed out into a sealed container attached to the milking unit. Then the milk was poured into a milk churn. All the churns were taken to the road and loaded onto a lorry which took the milk from the farm to the dairy. The machines saved time, but there was still a lot of manual work.

By the 1960s a group of machines in a milking parlour were connected, through pipes, to a central tank. The milk was automatically transferred to the tank, where it was stored and kept cool. Then it was pumped straight from the tank into the lorry.

A Milking a cow by hand

OVER TO YOU

1 Study the photos in **B**. List the ways that the Aireys' milking parlour:
  a cuts down on the need for labour
  b helps the cowman care for the cows, keeping them clean and fit
  c means that more cows can be kept on the farm
  d increases profits and also helps cut the price of milk for the customer.

2 Farms can be described as:
  - **extensive** – they cover a large area, but do not use much labour, machinery and equipment
  - **capital intensive** – they cover a fairly small area, but use a lot of machinery and equipment
  - **labour intensive** – they cover a fairly small area, but use a lot of labour.

  Which of these three phrases best describes the Aireys' farm? Explain your answer.

3 Read factfile **C**. Then choose the term from the 'Key Words!' box which **best** describes Black Moss.

  Explain your answer.

C Factfile on Black Moss Farm

Black Moss Farm covers 136 hectares. Of this:
  - 20 ha are rough grassland
  - 85 ha are improved grazing
  - 31 ha are used to grow barley to feed to the cattle.

The farm has 150 cows that are mature enough to produce milk. There are also 1 bull, 50 female calves, and 40 heifers (immature cows).
Of the farm's income:
  - about 85% comes from selling milk
  - about 10% comes from selling animals
  - about 5% comes from letting out land for grazing sheep in winter.

4 Think ahead to the year 2020! Imagine that Black Moss is still a dairy farm. Wayne and Adam are in charge now. It is time to invest in a new milking parlour. They want to make it even bigger and more efficient.

Suggest what the 2020 milking parlour might be like.

In the Airey's new milking parlour **B**

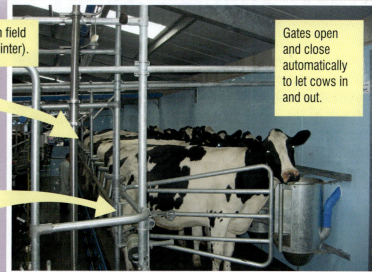

Cows brought in from field (summer) or shed (winter).

Gates open and close automatically to let cows in and out.

Cowman enters each cow's number on computer.

Computer keeps a record of each cow's milk yield and calculates how much food she needs.

Computer also helps cowman to check health of each cow. It shows when she is ready to stop milking, and to become pregnant with her next calf.

Cowman can milk 14 cows at once. Fits units to cows' udders. He stands below cows, so is at a comfortable height.

Milk taken straight from parlour to sterile storage tank.

Two days' milk can be stored. Then it is pumped directly into a collection lorry.

Computer controls cooling and washing of tank.

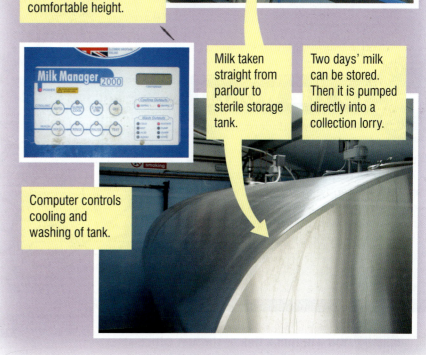

Key Words!

Arable
Growing and selling crops, mainly cereals, like wheat, barley, oats and sugar beet.

Pastoral
Growing mainly grass, which is eaten by animals like cows and sheep. The farmer's income comes from selling the animals, or products like milk or wool.

Dairy
A pastoral farm which mainly keeps cattle.

Mixed
A farm that does not specialise, but which sells some crops and also keeps some animals.

How is farming affected by the environment?

We need moderate summer temperatures, warm enough for the grass to grow, but not too hot or all the moisture evaporates.

We need moderate rainfall all through the year. If it is too wet, the cattle make the soil muddy and ruin the grass. If it is too dry the grass just doesn't grow.

Dairy cattle need luscious grass. This grows best on flat land, which holds some moisture in the soil but is quite well-drained. Cattle are not like sheep, which can live on steep slopes with poor-quality grass.

We like warm springs and warm autumns. That means that the grass has a longer growing season and we can keep the cattle outside longer. They keep fitter and seem happier, so they give more milk. It's also less work for us than feeding them indoors.

A John and Emmie outside the milking parlour

PASSPORT TO THE WORLD

Knowing and understanding something about climate statistics is useful in many jobs. Obviously it helps farmers and travel agents, and people involved in the transport industry. Who else do you think it helps? Why not visit the Met Office homepage on the internet? It is full of news and facts and ideas about weather in the UK and the rest of the world.

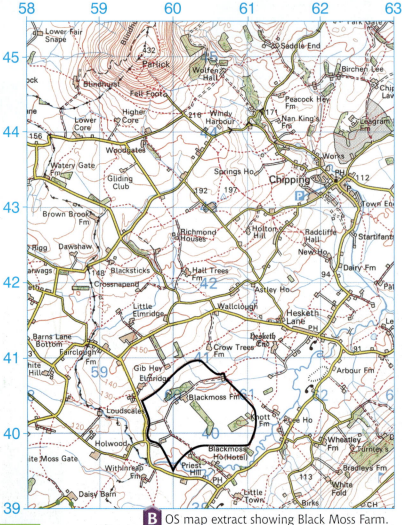

B OS map extract showing Black Moss Farm. Scale 1:50 000
© Crown Copyright

WEBLINKS You will find a link to the Met Office at www.nelsonthornes.com/horizons/weblinks

OVER TO YOU

1 Look at photo **D**. It shows part of Black Moss Farm. Describe the land. Say how it is being used.

2 Look at the OS map extract **B**. What else does this tell you about the land on the farm? You could refer to height, gradient, drainage and any other features that you can see.

3 The land in grid square 6239 is not very suitable for farming. Why? How has it been used instead?

4 Now describe the land in grid square 5944. Refer to the same details as in activity 2.

5 Explain why the land at Black Moss Farm is better for dairy farming than the land in 5944.

6 The land in grid square 5944 is poor-quality farmland. It cannot be used for dairy cattle, but other animals are kept here.

Suggest what kind of farm animals are suited to the conditions here. Explain your answer.

7 a Study the climate graphs **C**. For the Longridge area, work out:
- total rainfall
- season of most rainfall
- season of least rainfall
- temperature of warmest month
- temperature of coolest month.

b Compare the climate graphs for Longridge and London. Why is the climate near Longridge more suitable for dairy farming?

8 On average, the temperature on top of Parlick (GR 596451) is 3°C colder and has about 10% more rainfall each month than at Black Moss Farm.

Why is the climate at Black Moss more suitable than at Parlick, for dairy farming?

D View looking east from 598402

C

Rainfall (mm)   Temperature (°C)

Climate of Longridge

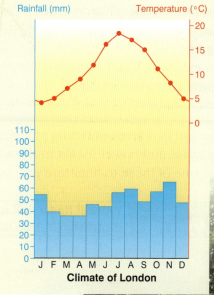

Rainfall (mm)   Temperature (°C)

Climate of London

What is secondary industry?

Many of the things that you buy seem simple. It is easy to take them for granted. But it is worth looking more closely at some of them to see how they are made. It often turns out that the manufacture of everyday articles is a complicated process. It usually takes place in factories. Diagram *A* summarises what takes place in a factory.

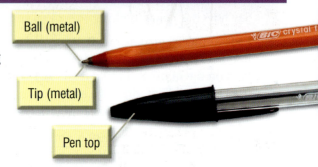
Ball (metal)
Tip (metal)
Pen top

Factories are usually built in places where costs are low. For instance, Norsk Hydro is a Norwegian company. It makes fertilisers using cheap power that comes from a hydro-electric plant. Electricity is generated by water flowing down a steep mountain-side into a valley.

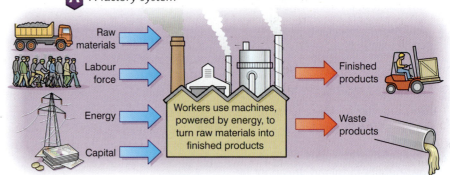
A A factory system

Raw materials
Labour force
Energy
Capital
Workers use machines, powered by energy, to turn raw materials into finished products
Finished products
Waste products

You can find some stunning pictures of Norsk Hydro's factories and power plants in Norway. Perhaps you could use one of these to illustrate your work.

WEBLINKS You will find a link to Norsk Hydro at www.nelsonthornes.com/horizons/weblinks

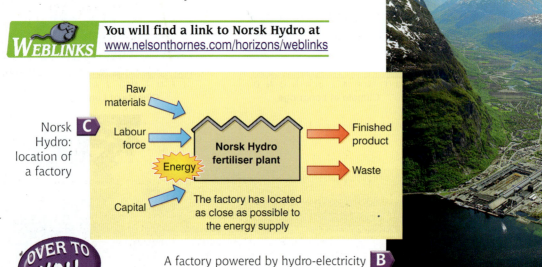
Norsk Hydro: location of a factory **C**

Raw materials
Labour force
Energy
Capital
Norsk Hydro fertiliser plant
The factory has located as close as possible to the energy supply
Finished product
Waste

A factory powered by hydro-electricity **B**

OVER TO YOU

1 Factory owners try to cut their costs. Where would be the best place to build:

   a a factory making frozen fish fingers → (its main raw material has to be processed while it is still very fresh)

   b a factory making cheap clothes → (it needs a large workforce, who have sewing skills but do not demand high wages)

   c a factory making fresh bread and cakes → (if the products are not sold on the day they are baked, they lose a lot of value)

2 Draw your own diagrams, like diagram **C**, to illustrate your answers to activity 1.

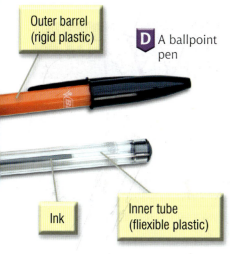

Outer barrel (rigid plastic)

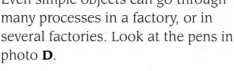

D A ballpoint pen

Ink

Inner tube (fliexible plastic)

Even simple objects can go through many processes in a factory, or in several factories. Look at the pens in photo **D**.

Each pen costs about 20p. Make a list of all its parts. They were put together in an assembly plant. What had to happen to make those parts before they reached the assembly plant? Some of them, like the 'barrel' of the pen and the pen top, had to be moulded. The plastic was heated and poured into the mould. This made the correct shape. Then all the parts – and the ink – were brought together, fitted, checked, packed, and sent to market.

So where did the plastic come from? There are lots of different types, all made from different combinations of chemicals. Each type of plastic in your pen was manufactured in a chemical plant. The chemicals were probably made from crude oil. The oil came from the rocks beneath the ground and was broken down into different elements, then these were put together again in different combinations to make the plastic... and so on.

If it is so complicated, why is this pen so cheap?

Two reasons are:
- the use of many machines means that labour costs are kept as low as possible
- mass-production of many thousands of pens means that the cost of machinery etc. is shared among all the pens, so each one costs very little.

Diagram **E** is a very simplified version of the manufacture of that pen.

Key Words!

Components
Parts that are made in one factory and then taken to another factory to be assembled to make a finished product.

Assembly plant
It takes parts from other factories and puts them together to make a finished product.

Assembly line
This is a part of a factory where products move along a conveyor belt. As they go along the line other parts are added. Each person on the assembly line has his/her own specialised task. This type of manufacturing is called **mass production**.

Mechanisation
In a factory it means using more and more machines, and fewer and fewer workers. In MEDCs it is a way of cutting costs because labour costs are usually very high.

3 Find another simple object that you use in school, or at home, or when travelling. (Keep it simple!)
  a List the raw materials that went into it.
  b List the manufacturing processes that went into it.
  c Draw a flow diagram to illustrate its manufacture.

4 Think about a factory near to your school or home.
  a What does it make?
  b Find out about its raw materials, energy supply, workforce and markets.
  c Describe its location.
  d Why was this a good place to build the factory?
  e Is it still a good location?

E Manufacture of a ballpoint pen

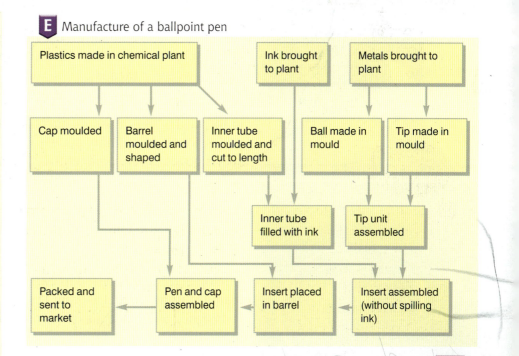

Where is the UK's secondary industry going?

On pages 94–95 you saw how industry tries to cut its costs by replacing workers with machines – mechanisation.

Another way to cut labour costs is by moving production from places where labour is expensive to places where it is cheaper. Many companies are based in richer, more economically developed countries (MEDCs). They have moved some of their production to poorer, less economically developed countries (LEDCs). There are a number of reasons for this – see table **A**.

Of course there are still advantages for locating some parts of manufacturing industry in MEDCs – see table **B**.

In LEDCs:
wages are lower
safety laws are often less strict which makes factories cheaper to run
raw materials and resources, such as electricity, are often less expensive
labour laws, to protect workers' rights, are often less strict
there are fewer unions, with less strength to negotiate good conditions for workers.

A

In MEDCs:
the workforce is usually better educated and trained
it may be useful to be close to the market, so that the industry can respond quickly to changes in fashion and demand
transport costs to market may be lower, and transport times will be quicker
governments are often more stable, so companies can plan ahead more easily
there are many high-tech firms and university departments that firms can share new ideas with.

B

THINK ... again!

Is it right for UK companies to move factories and jobs to LEDCs to save money? If you answer 'No', you then have to ask yourself, 'Would I pay more for clothes etc. that were made in the UK with more expensive labour?'

C

Manufacturing case study – sports goods

You can see how companies use different countries around the world for different parts of the manufacturing process by studying another everyday object – a tennis racquet.

Dunlop Slazenger is one of the leading manufacturers of sports equipment in the world. They make racquets for all standards of player, from top professionals to ordinary players, in schools and parks. The market for sports goods is very competitive. If equipment is to sell well it must:

- be up to date, with all the latest technology
- be well designed, to look good as well as being practical
- present a good image, particularly being endorsed by top players
- be fashionable.

Dunlop Slazenger is based in Camberley, Surrey but they do not do any manufacturing there. Diagram **D** shows how – and where – a new racquet is designed and made, as quickly as possible, so that it can fit the needs listed above.

D

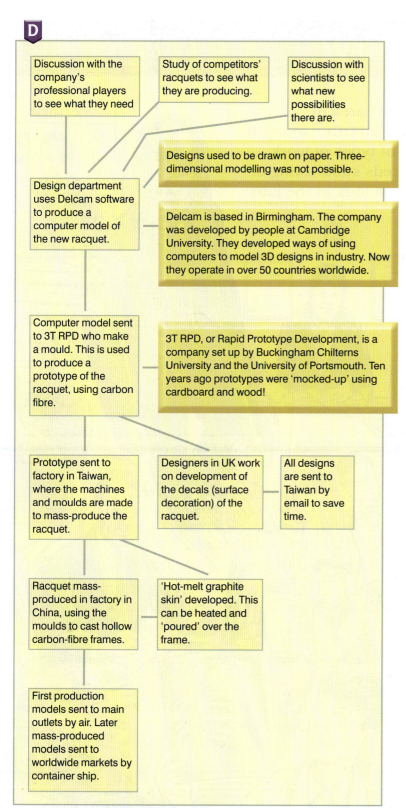

Discussion with the company's professional players to see what they need

Study of competitors' racquets to see what they are producing.

Discussion with scientists to see what new possibilities there are.

Designs used to be drawn on paper. Three-dimensional modelling was not possible.

Design department uses Delcam software to produce a computer model of the new racquet.

Delcam is based in Birmingham. The company was developed by people at Cambridge University. They developed ways of using computers to model 3D designs in industry. Now they operate in over 50 countries worldwide.

Computer model sent to 3T RPD who make a mould. This is used to produce a prototype of the racquet, using carbon fibre.

3T RPD, or Rapid Prototype Development, is a company set up by Buckingham Chilterns University and the University of Portsmouth. Ten years ago prototypes were 'mocked-up' using cardboard and wood!

Prototype sent to factory in Taiwan, where the machines and moulds are made to mass-produce the racquet.

Designers in UK work on development of the decals (surface decoration) of the racquet.

All designs are sent to Taiwan by email to save time.

Racquet mass-produced in factory in China, using the moulds to cast hollow carbon-fibre frames.

'Hot-melt graphite skin' developed. This can be heated and 'poured' over the frame.

First production models sent to main outlets by air. Later mass-produced models sent to worldwide markets by container ship.

OVER TO YOU

1 Using a map of the world, with an enlargement of the UK:
  a mark, and label, all the places mentioned on the flow diagram
  b mark, and label, all the links between the places – use different colours to show e-links and physical links.

Note: shipping products to the worldwide market will mainly be to the USA, Europe, Australasia, Japan and other developed countries.

2 In 1995 it took at least six months to make a new racquet from design to production. Now it takes less than three months.
  a Why will this fast process have advantages for the company?
  b How do they use modern technology to speed up the process?

3 **a** Which parts of the manufacturing process are still based in the UK?
    What are the advantages, for the firm, of basing these processes here?
  b Which parts of the manufacturing take place in South East Asia?
    What are the advantages, for the firm, of basing these processes here?

4 How does this division of manufacturing affect:
  a the number of jobs for UK workers
  b the skills needed by UK workers
  c the rates of pay for UK workers?

5 Find out more about some of the companies involved in producing tennis racquets for Dunlop Slazenger. Visit the websites of some of these companies.

Key Words!

Prototype

The first 'try-out' version of a new product. It is used to test and improve the designer's ideas.

This manufacturing case study has links to understanding product design and industrial practice in Design & Technology.

You will find a link to companies like Dunlop Slazenger at www.nelsonthornes.com/horizons/weblinks

What is tertiary industry?

The service, or tertiary, sector is the biggest area of employment in the UK – and in most other MEDCs – today. It includes an enormous range and variety of types of work. Such a big group of employment types needs subdividing or sorting into separate classifications. Take a look at the jobs on these two pages.

OVER TO YOU

1 Think of about five different groups that you can divide service workers into. Then sort (or classify) the workers on this page into those different groups. For instance, you might have **health and education** as one of your groups. Then you might put **ambulance paramedic** in that group. Your teacher might give you some cards to sort out, to help you answer this question.

2 Did you have any left over who would not fit into any group? Which workers were they? Can you fit them in by having one more group, or do you need to start all over again with different groups?

3 Compare your groups with other people's groups. Which groups were the same? Which were different? Did you always make the same decisions about which workers went into which group? Were some of your answers *wrong* or were they just *differences of opinion*?

4 Now try to think of one or two more workers (not shown on these pages) who would fit into each of your groups.

5 'The service sector is large and varied. It dominates the employment structure in most developed countries.'

Do you agree with that statement?

Write it out and explain what you think about it.

A

CASHIER

What's new in tertiary industry?

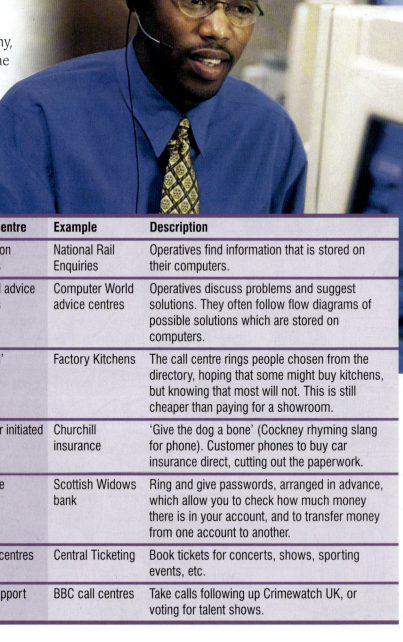

A

One reason for the growth of service employment in the UK is the growth of the call centre. They have spread rapidly since the mid-1990s. Call centres are a fairly new form of service employment.

A number of technological advances allowed these centres to develop. The advances included:

- computerisation of telephone exchange systems
- the development of satellite technology, which meant phones did not have to rely on transmission of messages through wires
- cable technology, so cables could carry many, many more messages than the old telephone wires had done
- the spread of mobile phones
- a fall in the price and an increase in the power of computers, allowing telephone operators to access information and to store it without using paper and filling in lots of forms.

There are many different types of call centre. Some of them are shown in table **B**.

B

C

Type of centre	Example	Description
Information providers	National Rail Enquiries	Operatives find information that is stored on their computers.
Technical advice providers	Computer World advice centres	Operatives discuss problems and suggest solutions. They often follow flow diagrams of possible solutions which are stored on computers.
'Cold call' telesales	Factory Kitchens	The call centre rings people chosen from the directory, hoping that some might buy kitchens, but knowing that most will not. This is still cheaper than paying for a showroom.
Customer initiated telesales	Churchill insurance	'Give the dog a bone' (Cockney rhyming slang for phone). Customer phones to buy car insurance direct, cutting out the paperwork.
Telephone banking	Scottish Widows bank	Ring and give passwords, arranged in advance, which allow you to check how much money there is in your account, and to transfer money from one account to another.
Booking centres	Central Ticketing	Book tickets for concerts, shows, sporting events, etc.
Media support	BBC call centres	Take calls following up Crimewatch UK, or voting for talent shows.

What are call centres like?

D

> We had a weekend break in London. I booked train tickets, made a hotel reservation and booked for a show by making three phone calls. We saved time and money. It was so easy.

> I'm really fed up of this 'cold calling'. It seems that they ring me about twice a week, just when I get home from work, to offer double glazing, or cheap insurance. I call them 'junk calls'!

> It's a good place to work. It's clean, modern and friendly. I got good training and there is a full support team to take over callers with difficult problems. The technicians see that our phone links, computer links, keyboards and screens all work efficiently. **Insurance claims worker**

> I think it's really impersonal, just talking to customers on the phone. It can get boring too. We're also under great pressure. Basic pay is poor and if we don't meet our sales quota we lose all our bonuses. **Telesales worker**

> We fit replacement windows. About half our jobs come from the call centre and about half from recommendations. Using the call centre means that we don't have the costs of a showroom on the High Street. **Company manager**

> We have one call centre that serves the whole country. This saves overheads. We located in the north-east partly because wage rates are lower here, but also because people find the Geordie accent friendly and are more likely to buy our product. We might have to relocate to India, though. Wage rates there are even lower, but people in the UK might have a problem with the accents. **Call centre manager**

WEBLINKS **You will find a link to find out more about call centres at** www.nelsonthornes.com/horizons/weblinks

OVER TO YOU

1. Carry out a quick survey to find out what types of call centres the people in your class have used. For example, you might have phoned a TV show or someone might have called 999.

2. Who benefits from the development of call centres?

   How do they bring benefits to:
   a customers
   b employers
   c workers?

3. Who loses from the development of call centres?

   How do they bring disadvantages to:
   a customers
   b employers
   c workers?

4. Read through your answers to activities 1 and 2 again.

   On balance, do you think that the growth of call centres in the last 15 years has been a good thing or a bad thing?

   Explain your answer.

5. Do you think that employment in call centres in the UK will go on increasing, or will it start to decline?

   Explain your answer.

Fantastic Facts

In 2003 there were 2100 UK call centres registered with the Call Centre Management Association. Some people feel that the number is at its peak now and that decline will soon set in as centres are moved to LEDCs – just as manufacturing moved in the late 20th century.

Where are we now?

On pages 86 and 87 you saw how the employment structure of the UK has changed over the last 40 years or so.

Check back to those pages and see what has happened to employment in:

- the primary sector
- the secondary sector
- the tertiary sector.

Now you must think about three **key questions**:

1 As any country develops, does its employment structure change?

2 Do more economically developed countries have a higher proportion of people employed in the tertiary sector?

3 Do less economically developed countries have a higher proportion of people employed in the primary and secondary sectors?

Use the information in table **A** to help you answer these questions.

A

	% of workforce (2002) in:			
	primary sector	secondary sector	tertiary sector	GNI/person (in thousand US$)
Australia	7	22	71	19.7
Brazil	37	11	52	2.9
China	39	27	34	0.9
India	69	7	24	0.5
Japan	7	27	66	33.5
Kenya	61	10	29	0.4
Mexico	43	15	42	5.9
Nigeria	56	9	35	0.3
Russia	12	37	51	2.1
Saudi Arabia	27	4	69	8.5
Spain	11	25	64	14.4
UK	4	26	70	25.3
USA	5	22	73	35.0

Key Words!

GNI/person

Gross National Income per person is a fairly new term which is replacing the old term Gross National Product (or GNP).

B

1 Write the name of each country listed in table **A** on a card, in the centre.

Write the figure for GNI in the top left corner of the card.

Write the figures for primary – secondary – tertiary employment across the bottom.

Card **C** has been done for you.

2 Divide the 13 cards into three piles. Put all the countries with similar incomes into the same pile.

3 Take your first pile and compare the percentage of people working in primary industry in each country. Is there any pattern? Are they all similar? Do any countries not fit the pattern?

At this point you could decide to move a card from one group into another.

4 Repeat activity 3 for each type of employment in each of the piles.

5 Use this information to try to answer the key questions 1–3 opposite. Then compare your answers with those of other people in the class.

6 **a** Write a summary of your findings on a copy of the world map **B**.

b Shade the countries to show which groups you put them in. Make sure that you add a key.

You could write your comments in boxes around the edge of your map and then add arrows to show which places you are referring to.

Extension task

7 Add located pie charts to your map. Draw a pie chart to illustrate the employment structure of one representative country from each group. Stick this over, or close to, that country on the map.

8 Look for pictures to illustrate the main types of employment in the different countries. Search the internet, or collect pictures from magazines and newspapers. Then stick these around your map.

9 **a** How do you predict work patterns will change in these countries over the next 20 years? Explain your answer.

b Explain how this might affect *you*.

C

$25.3 thousand per person

United Kingdom

Primary
4

Secondary
26

Tertiary
70

6 Exploring the UK

Is this the United Kingdom?

Where are we going?

In this unit you will learn to ...

- understand why the people of the UK are culturally diverse
- distinguish between UK climate and weather
- evaluate bias in images of the UK
- develop an awareness of the place of the UK in the world.

The United Kingdom, or UK, is where 59 million of us live. But how well do we know our country, and how it got to be like it is today? If you asked 100 people around the world what the UK is like, you could get 100 different answers. The same would be true if you asked people in the UK!

You will have a mental image of the UK based on many different sources of information. But how accurate are your current perceptions?

By the time you get to the end of this unit, your ideas may have changed!

Images of the UK

G

H

OVER TO
YOU

1 a Write down:
- five of the most important things you know about the UK
- five words you would use to describe the UK.

b Compare these with your partner or with the rest of the class. Which are the most common choices? Why do you think that might be?

2 Study the photos **A–H**. Each image is taken from a promotional video about the UK for visitors to the country.

a Think of three words to describe each picture (either what you see or how it makes you feel).

b For each image, say whether you think the image will attract tourists or business people to the UK. Write your answer like this:

A = *tourist.*

c Write a sentence to explain why you think your choice of visitor will be attracted by what the image shows.

3 Use copies of at least five of these images (**A–H**) to make a video storyboard. You need to write a voice-over to be narrated to visitors, telling them what the UK is like. You might want to think about the kind of music to be played in the background.

4 Draw an opinion line like the one below. Write down along your line the letters of the images, arranging them according to how much or how little they represent your idea of the UK.

5 Write a paragraph to explain why you have chosen the top two and the bottom two as the most and least representative of your UK. Think about how the following factors affect your views: knowledge, personal experiences, where you live.

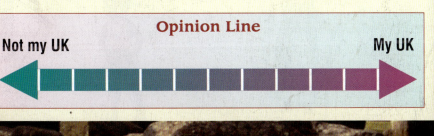

Opinion Line

Not my UK ⟵ ⟶ My UK

Fantastic Facts

Britain is just under 1000 km long, from the south coast to the extreme north of Scotland, and just under 500 km across at the widest point.

The biggest lake in the UK is Lough Neagh in Northern Ireland at 396 km².

There are 17 World Heritage Sites in the UK, including Hadrian's Wall, Stonehenge, the Giant's Causeway, and Edinburgh's Old and New Towns.

Birmingham (UK), has more miles of canals than Venice.

What do we mean by the UK?

Our island is changing. It always has been. Only 10 000 years ago you could have walked over a land bridge to France before the ice melted and the sea rose. Just 500 years ago Henry VIII had a naval port on the coast at Rye, but now it is 3 miles inland! We know that the shape of the land is changing gradually all the time – but the borders of the countries that make up the UK can change much more rapidly.

Borders are boundaries between countries, which you can see on political maps. They may reflect changes in natural features like hills or rivers, which you can see on a physical map, but you may not be able to see a border on the ground unless it is marked by a barrier or a sign. These boundaries have been the cause of death and dispute over the last 2000 years. Why do they change? What do we feel about 'our' side of a border? These are important questions.

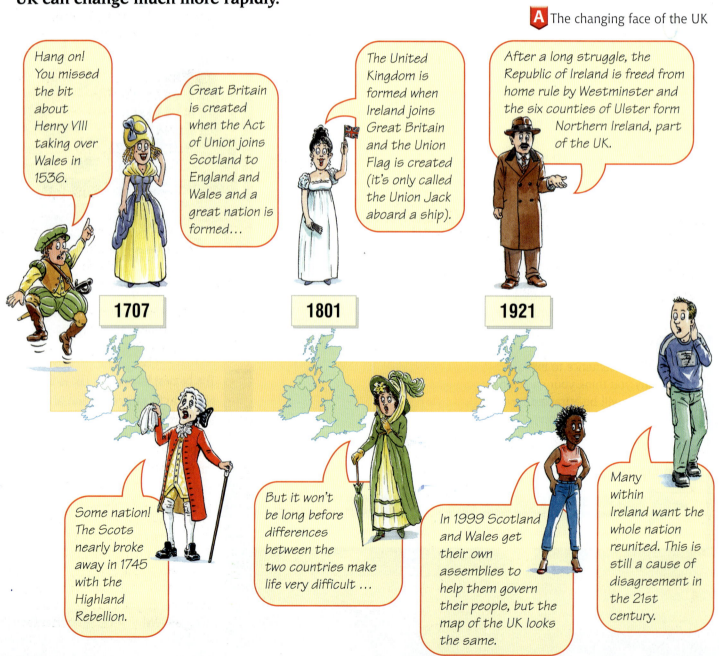

A The changing face of the UK

Hang on! You missed the bit about Henry VIII taking over Wales in 1536.

Great Britain is created when the Act of Union joins Scotland to England and Wales and a great nation is formed…

The United Kingdom is formed when Ireland joins Great Britain and the Union Flag is created (it's only called the Union Jack aboard a ship).

After a long struggle, the Republic of Ireland is freed from home rule by Westminster and the six counties of Ulster form Northern Ireland, part of the UK.

1707

1801

1921

Some nation! The Scots nearly broke away in 1745 with the Highland Rebellion.

But it won't be long before differences between the two countries make life very difficult …

In 1999 Scotland and Wales get their own assemblies to help them govern their people, but the map of the UK looks the same.

Many within Ireland want the whole nation reunited. This is still a cause of disagreement in the 21st century.

B What is the UK?

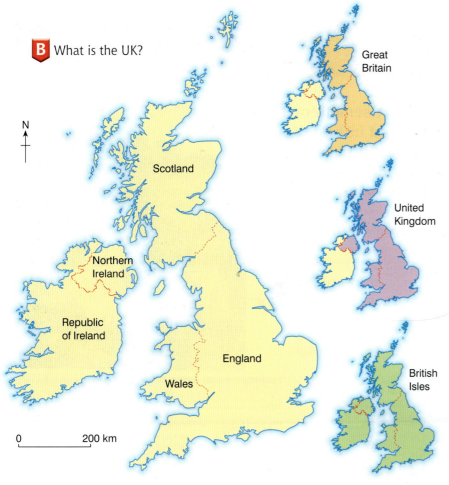

N

0   200 km

Great
Britain

United
Kingdom

British
Isles

Scotland

Northern
Ireland

Republic
of Ireland

England

Wales

C Facts about the British Isles

Country	Area (km²)	Population (millions)	Population density (people/km²)
England	130 000	48.5	373.1
Scotland	77 000	5.0	
Wales	21 000	3.0	
Northern Ireland	13 500	1.5	
Republic of Ireland	69 000	3.5	

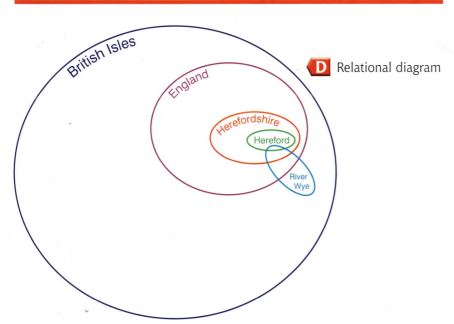

British Isles

England

Herefordshire

Hereford

River
Wye

D Relational diagram

1 What is a border? Give an example in your answer.

2 a Copy table **C**. Work out the population density for each country. *Hint*: The answer for England is worked out on page 26.

  b Which country is the most densely populated?

  c Which country is the most sparsely populated?

  d Why do you think some UK countries are more densely populated than others? Use pages 26–27 and front cover resource **C** to help you.

3 a What is the average (mean) population density for the UK?

  b Which of the following has an average population density of about 190 km²?

The British Isles

Great Britain   England

4 Write a short paragraph explaining the differences in population, area and population density for the UK, Great Britain and the British Isles.

5 a Arrange these places into a relational diagram like the one in diagram **D**:
- East Anglia
- Norfolk
- England
- United Kingdom
- British Isles
- Norwich
- Great Britain.

  b Add your own town, county and region to your diagram.

  c Use an atlas to name one large river and one upland area in England, Scotland, Wales and Northern Ireland.

  d Write down the most important relationship you can see in your diagram. Why is it so important?

What is your UK really like?

Every time you look at a magazine, advertisement or TV programme, you are looking at images and information chosen by someone else for a reason. *Bias* occurs when the provider of the image emphasises some aspects of the available information but leaves others out. Even with well-balanced sources, we can be biased in the way we interpret them, perhaps only accepting the bits that fit in with what we know already.

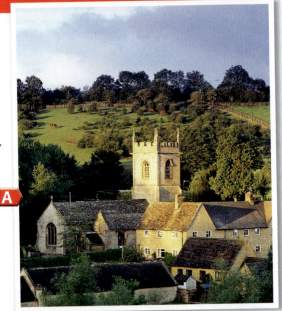

A

Images that show predictable views are said to be **stereotypes**. They are meant to simplify or summarise a more complex picture and may guide the way we think. Image **B** is a stereotype view of rural England from a Second World War poster. It summed up what the country was meant to be about and what men were being asked to fight for. Any British soldier seeing it, even if they had never been to the countryside, would instantly recognise it as Britain.

B

Your **BRITAIN** · fight for it now

Holiday cottage to let

In a superb rural location, this attractive thatched cottage, with its own large garden, is just 6 miles from the beautiful East Devon Heritage Coast. Adjoining the owner's 16th-century farmhouse, it has been sympathetically converted from a barn to offer comfortable and individually styled accommodation. Excellent coastal walks and attractive towns to visit nearby, including Honiton (4 miles), famous for its lace and antique shops, Sidmouth, Branscombe and Seaton. Cathedral city of Exeter 20 miles. Riding in village. Pub 1½ miles. Entrance hall. Spacious living/dining-room with wood-burning stove in stone surround. Cottage-style kitchen. Shower room/WC. First floor: Double bedroom with handmade iron bed. Twin-bedded room. Bathroom/WC.
* Full CH and elec. incl. * Wood-burning stove (fuel incl.)
* Parking (for 2 cars) * Shops 4 miles * TV * Video * CD player
* Auto wm * M/wave * Fridge/freezer * Cot * Large garden with sitting-out area and furniture * Barbecue * Duvets with linen and towels * Friday to Friday

C

OVER TO YOU

Imagine you are a visitor to the UK and are thinking of staying in the village shown in photo **A** for a year.

1 What impression of the villages do you get from sources **A**, **B** and **C**?
   a Who are these pictures meant to be seen by?
   b Who is responsible for creating them?
   c Why might they be biased?
   d Which could be said to be a stereotype? Why?

2 Say how your views are changed by reading sources **D**, **E** and **F**?

3 Suggest which extra information would be useful to have before you would consider moving to that village to live.

4 Read the sources **G** and **H**. For each one write a short paragraph to explain what impression you think the writer was trying to give about the UK countryside.

5 What kind of images do you think best represent your town? Plan a one-page flyer with suitable images to present your town as you see it. Think about the message you are trying to convey. Consider how similar or different it might be to a flyer put out by your local council.

Key Words!

Stereotype

A corny, predictable image used to simplify a more complex reality. If when someone says 'Scottish' you think of someone wearing a kilt, a sporran and a tam-o'-shanter on their head, you've just conjured up a stereotype. It doesn't represent the average Scot and can easily offend.

Images from rural Britain

D

> I was born in this village and I can't recall it being in the state it is today. I don't know if it's the incomers with their teenagers or the tourists. If people can't cherish something as lovely as this old village, then there must be something really wrong with the world.

A recent survey found that:

- lawlessness was threatening to destroy the quality of village life in England and Wales
- 71% of rural villages have no regular police presence
- the growth of CCTV in urban areas seems to be pushing crime out to the countryside
- rural dwellers feel more isolated and vulnerable to crime, and are worried about rural unemployment and the impact that rocketing fuel bills have on their high transport costs.

F Press report of rural crime

G From *Notes from a Small Island* by Bill Bryson, an American travel writer

E

> My mum and dad wanted to live here, not me. It's so boring for people of my age. There's nothing to do and nowhere to go unless you've got a car. Anything you do for a bit of fun has the locals complaining to the police – wherever **they** are.

... Barnstaple used to be a major rail interchange, with three stations, but now there is just the one with its infrequent pootling services to Exeter, and a bus station ... I went into the bus station and found two women sitting in an office. I asked them about the buses to Minehead, about 30 miles to the east along the coast. They looked at me as if I'd asked for connections to Tierra del Fuego.
'Oh, you wont be gittin to Moinhead this toim of year, you won't be,' said one.
'No buses to Moinhead arter firrrrst of Octobaaarrrr,' chimed in the second one.
'What about Lynton and Lynmouth?'
They snorted at my naivety. This was England. This was 1994.
'Porlock?'
Snort
'Dunster?'
Snort
The best they could suggest was that I take a bus to Bideford and see if I could catch another bus on from there.
'They may be runnin the Scarrrrrrlet Loin out of Bideforrrrrd, they may be, oi they may be, they may – but can't be sartin.' .... I thanked them and departed.

Writing inspired by travelling through the British countryside **H**

Adlestrop *by Edward Thomas*

Yes. I remember Adlestrop –
The name, because one afternoon
Of heat the express-train drew up there
Unwontedly. It was late June.

The steam hissed. Someone cleared his throat.
No one left and no one came
On the bare platform. What I saw
Was Adlestrop – only the name.

And willows, willow-herb, and grass,
And meadowsweet, and haycocks dry,
No whit less still and lonely fair
Than the high cloudlets in the sky.

And for that minute a blackbird sang
Close by, and round him, mistier,
Farther and farther, all the birds
Of Oxfordshire and Gloucestershire.

 **Links to...** Understanding how people view images of places helps us to understand how some places are favoured by tourists. This idea is investigated further in *Horizons 2*.

How did we get to the UK?

The last great ice sheets began to retreat from Britain 10 000 years ago. Until 7000 years ago there were very few people living in Britain. So where did we all come from?

We are the **descendants** of **immigrants** who have migrated here at different stages since those times. Map **A** shows just some of the people who moved to Britain, the times when they started to arrive, and why they may have left their homelands.

1 Map **A** does not show where UK migrants came from very clearly. On your own copy of the map, re-order the information so that the arrow directions show more closely where in the world the immigrants came from.

2 Colour code the arrows by shading them using the scheme in table **B**.

B Colour coding the causes of migration

Reason	To find new land	To find work	To take over	To escape persecution
Colour	green	orange	red	blue

3 Which continent do most of the migrants seem to have come from? Suggest why this is so.

4 Find out what is the most common reason for coming to Britain. Suggest why that is the case.

5 In which century do most migrants seem to have arrived? Suggest why.

6 India, Pakistan, Bangladesh, Uganda and some of the Caribbean islands were once British colonies and are still part of the Commonwealth. Why might this have helped migrants from these places to move to the UK?

7 Write a paragraph to explain why British people no longer think of themselves as being Romans, Saxons or Vikings.

1066: Normans from France conquer Britain.

43 AD: Romans arrive from Italy and take control.

1999: Kurds, Kosovans and other Eastern Europeans flee from war-torn countries.

From 1960s: Irish people come to find work.

1945 onwards: Poles, Italians and Latvians are invited by the British government to fill jobs.

Key Words!

Colony

A country that is controlled by another, more powerful, uninvited country. Colonisation often involves the exploitation of the weaker country.

 This work on the UK helps to develop a better understanding of many of the population and migration issues in Unit 2.

A Where are your descendants from?

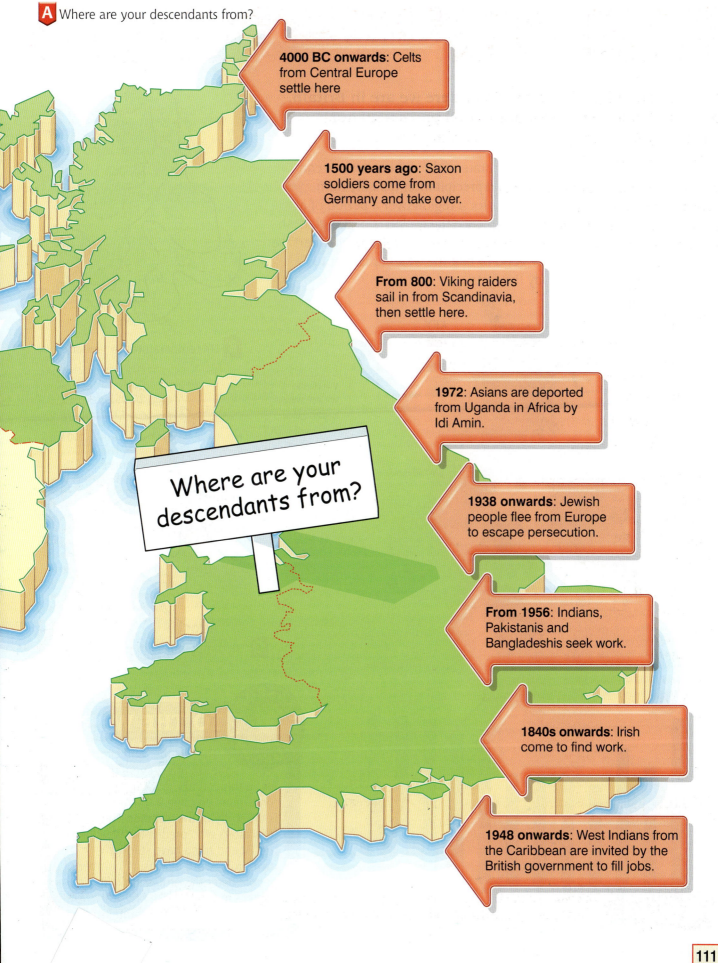

4000 BC onwards: Celts from Central Europe settle here

1500 years ago: Saxon soldiers come from Germany and take over.

From 800: Viking raiders sail in from Scandinavia, then settle here.

1972: Asians are deported from Uganda in Africa by Idi Amin.

Where are your descendants from?

1938 onwards: Jewish people flee from Europe to escape persecution.

From 1956: Indians, Pakistanis and Bangladeshis seek work.

1840s onwards: Irish come to find work.

1948 onwards: West Indians from the Caribbean are invited by the British government to fill jobs.

What is the weather like?

Our weather varies according to where we are in Britain. It can affect the way we work, travel and spend our leisure time.

The **weather** means the day-to-day state of the atmosphere. It can include temperature, wind, cloud and precipitation (usually rain). **Climate** means the average weather for a region over a period of at least 30 years. The UK does not experience the cyclones of Bangladesh or the searing heat of Jordan, yet we are obsessed with the weather! We all have an opinion about how good or bad the weather is, but to understand it we need to study the facts.

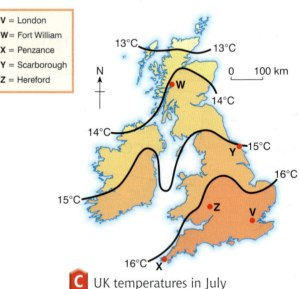

B UK temperatures in January

UK annual precipitation

A ▶

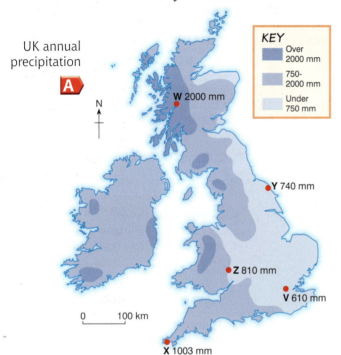

KEY
	Over 2000 mm
	750-2000 mm
	Under 750 mm

V = London
W = Fort William
X = Penzance
Y = Scarborough
Z = Hereford

C UK temperatures in July

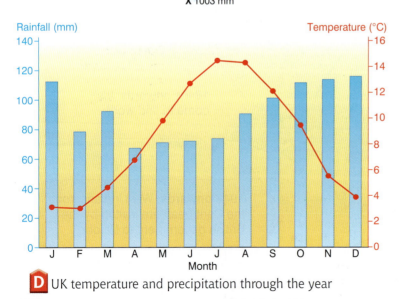

D UK temperature and precipitation through the year

TO THE WORLD

The weather and climate of the UK affect every aspect of life in this country (as you have seen for farmers on page 92). **Meteorology** is the study of the weather. The forecasters who predict the weather on the TV and radio have studied meteorology. An increasing number of people enter the profession with degrees in subjects like physical geography and environmental studies.

1 Fact or opinion? Judge these statements about the weather maps **B** and **C** opposite, and say if they are **fact** or **opinion**. Give reasons for your answers.

  a In July, Hereford is 2 degrees warmer than Fort William.

  b In January, Penzance is warmer than London by at least 10 degrees.

  c Scarborough is at least 2 degrees colder than London in January.

2 Look at diagram **E** below and try to work out the exact point on their journey that Alton and Kieron might have sent the texts marked A–E.

  a Mark the letters on a simple copy of the diagram. For each one say why you put it there. Write a paragraph to link the key words and the texts.

  b Look up these words in the Glossary on pages 126–127:

    condensation

    evaporation   **precipitation**

    Add these to your diagram in the place you think they best fit. Explain why you have placed them there.

3 Use all the information on these two pages to test the following hypotheses. You must say why they are true or false, giving examples from these pages. The weather forecaster's comments in the 'Remember…' box here may help you to explain your answers.

  a It is usually warmer in the south than in the north.

  b It is warmer in the uplands than in the lowlands.

  c The summer is colder than the winter.

  d It is wetter in the west than in the east.

  e It is drier in uplands than in lowlands.

  f There is more rainfall in the summer than in the winter.

OVER TO YOU

Remember …

The weather forecaster knows that:

- a warm ocean current called the North Atlantic Drift (Gulf Stream) keeps the west coast warmer than the east coast in winter
- for every 100 metres you gain in height, temperature drops by 1°C
- the greater the distance from the equator, the colder it gets.

WEBLINKS You will find a link to the BBC Weatherwise website at www.nelsonthornes.com/horizons/weblinks

Alton and Kieron are hiking from the seaside to the summit of Scafell. They are texting messages to their mate back in Liverpool. Which part of the trek do you think these texts will have been made from?

A
> Drying out and some sun at last.
>
> Options   Back

B
> A bit sunny and cloudy but warm here at the coast. Humid despite the sea breeze.
>
> Options   Back

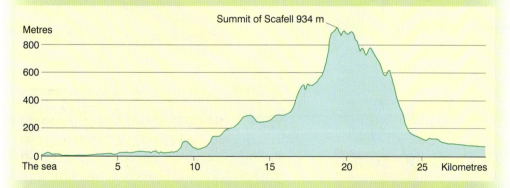

C
> Much cloudier now, I think it's going to rain...
>
> Options   Back

D
> Further inland now and cloudier. Shorts are too cool! Wish I'd brought my trousers...
>
> Options   Back

E
> Total cloud cover, I'm soaked and freezing!
>
> Options   Back

E Does upland mean wetland? A cross-section through Scafell

Why is the weather so changeable?

The day-to-day changes in our weather are a result of the location of the British Isles. In particular, the fact that we are on the edge of a continent means that we are exposed to different influences on the weather.

We are affected by five major air masses that bring different kinds of weather, depending on what time of year they arrive (map **A**). Two types of weather system affect Britain:

- High pressure (anticyclones) brings settled weather and clear, drier air, giving us sunny summer days but cold winter days and nights.
- Low pressure (depressions) often brings rain, cloud and wind to the British Isles. They are responsible for much of our very changeable weather.

A lot of our weather comes in from the west and much is created by weather **fronts**. Where warm and cold air meet at a front, the heavier cold air wraps around the lighter warm air causing it to rise, cool and form clouds and rain. A depression takes only 1 to 3 days to pass over us – but there are always more on the way!

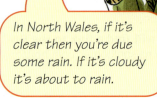

If you don't like the weather – wait 15 minutes and it will have changed. It can be four seasons in one day on Skye!

In North Wales, if it's clear then you're due some rain. If it's cloudy it's about to rain.

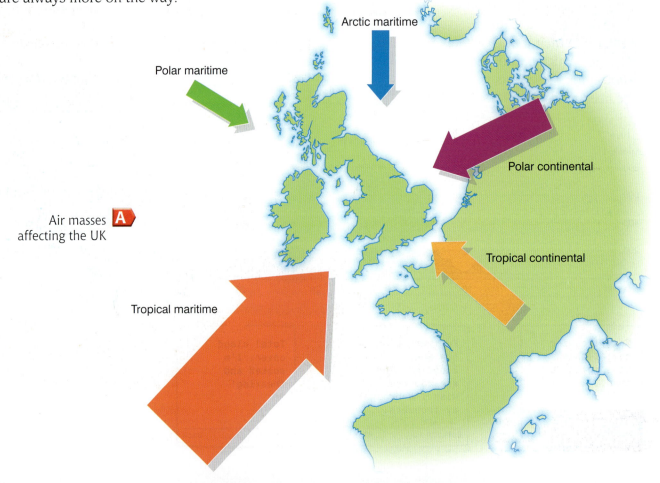

Air masses **A** affecting the UK

Arctic maritime

Polar maritime

Polar continental

Tropical continental

Tropical maritime

114

1 a What kind of weather does high pressure bring to the UK?

b What kind of weather does low pressure bring to the UK?

2 Map **A** shows the air masses affecting Britain. The width of the arrows tells us how often the weather comes from that direction (which means if the arrow is wider, the weather comes from there more often).

a Copy and complete the following statements:

i The two most common air masses affecting the UK are ...... and .... The weather they bring ......

ii In winter when there is an easterly wind ......

iii Air coming from the south in winter ......

iv When the weather is mainly from the west ......

b Add at least one more statement yourself.

3 Label a simple copy of diagram **B** with the following statements:
- This is where the advancing warm air meets the cold air.
- As it is pushes up the warm front it cools, condenses and forms clouds.
- Rain falls over a wide area.

4 When a depression passes over the UK, there is usually a warm front followed by a cold front (diagram **B**).

a Write a brief weather forecast for tomorrow. The warm front of the depression shown in the diagram will cross

Plymouth at 6 am and London at 9 pm. You must mention the following:

OVER TO YOU

rain   cloud

wind strength

b Which city do you think will receive the most rain during the day? Why?

5 Write a report for the next Year 7 classes on 'Why the UK has changeable weather'. Try to make your report as complete as you can. You can test how complete it is by checking it with your partner's version. Award yourself one point for each fact you both include, but lose one for every correct fact your partner got that you didn't.

B Cross-section of a depression

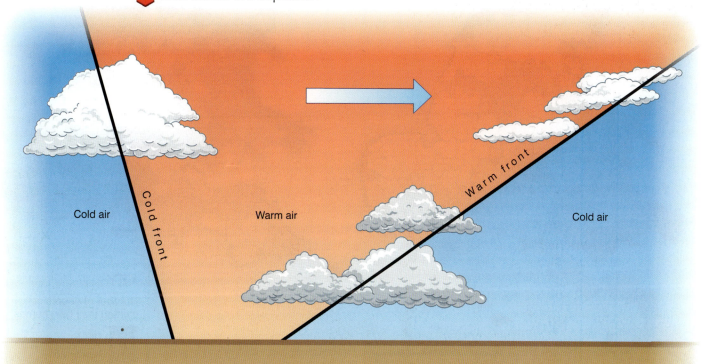

Cold air   Cold front   Warm air   Warm front   Cold air

 **Links to...** You will learn more about weather and climate in *Horizons 2*.

A kingdom united or divided?

We already know that England, Scotland, Wales and Northern Ireland have different areas, populations, customs and even languages. But are there other differences in the UK that are hidden, even within one country?

The maps on these pages show information mapped out by local authority areas for England and Wales. Geographers need to be able to see **patterns** of inequality. We need to describe those patterns and then find reasons for the differences within the kingdom.

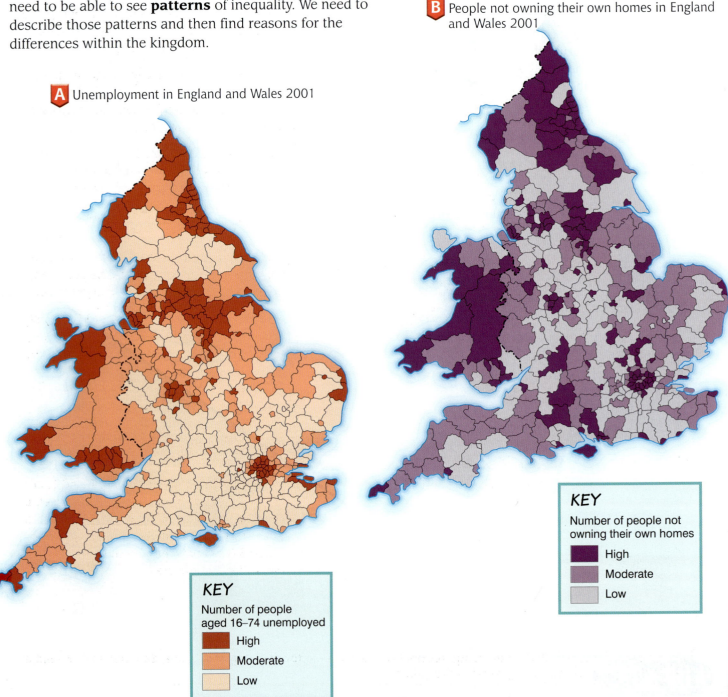

A Unemployment in England and Wales 2001

B People not owning their own homes in England and Wales 2001

KEY

Number of people aged 16–74 unemployed

- High
- Moderate
- Low

KEY

Number of people not owning their own homes

- High
- Moderate
- Low

OVER TO YOU

1 a What is meant by these words? Unemployment, Home ownership, Health
b Why do you think it is important for governments to know about these issues?

2 Look at map **A**. The dark red areas show parts of England and Wales where unemployment is highest.
a Describe the distribution of unemployment in England and Wales. Use words like: *north, south, east, west* and *north-west*.
b Now look at map **A** on page 26, showing population density and the location of major urban areas. Is the pattern of unemployment similar to or different from the pattern for rural/urban areas? Why might this be?

3 Study map **B**. Are there any similarities or differences between the patterns for home ownership and unemployment? Suggest reasons for what you have found.

4 What links would you predict between poor health and what you know so far about unemployment and home ownership? Write down your prediction, e.g.
Areas with poorer health are ...

5 Study map **C**. Describe the pattern you see on this map. Then compare it with the other two. Does this appear to fit in with your prediction?

6 Which of the following indicators do you think might have a link with the patterns you have seen so far? Which might not? Suggest reasons for your predictions.
a University degree
b Number of holidays per year
c Crime
d Number of football teams
e Visits to the cinema

7 Find your own region on maps **A**, **B** and **C**, or find the relevant information on the internet. Do you think they show what you would expect, or do they seem very different from the place you know? Suggest how the data could be misleading for your area.

C State of people's health in England and Wales 2001

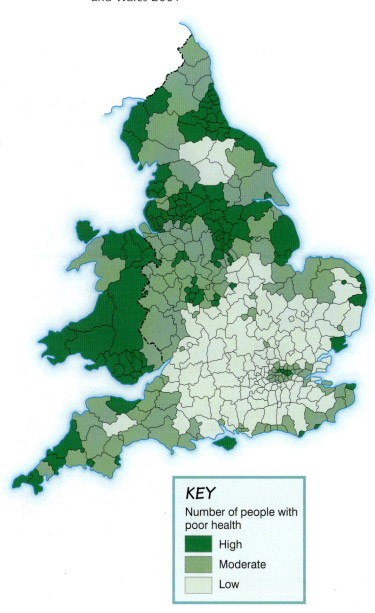

KEY
Number of people with poor health

- High
- Moderate
- Low

WEBLINKS You will find links giving information on census returns in England, Wales, Scotland and Ireland at www.nelsonthornes.com/horizons/weblinks

Internet UK – what do we do?

Investigating your own town will enable you to compare it with the UK patterns and averages we looked at on pages 116–117. The information you need is already there, on the internet. There's no limit to what you can find out, but the best way to investigate is to think of the right questions before you start. If you know *what* you want to find out, you will waste less time when searching.

Log on to the government National Statistics website to find out about local unemployment, earnings, health and home ownership. Try typing in your postcode or the name of your nearest town to narrow down your search.

You can find other areas of information to extend your search and you will also be given UK averages to compare with. Look up 'Employment' to see what kind of jobs people do in your town.

Many local newspapers have websites you can search for local firms and businesses. Figure **B** shows one example.

WEBLINKS You will find links to the government National Statistics website, and to other sites giving information about house prices and services, at www.nelsonthornes.com/horizons/weblinks

OVER TO YOU

1 a Name at least six jobs done by people you know. Group them under the headings:

primary   tertiary

secondary

You can look back to page 84 for help. Your teacher might do a class survey to pool your findings.

b Find out the total number of jobs in each group. Work out the percentage of jobs that are primary, secondary and tertiary.

2 Diagram **C** shows the national figures for different types of employment. Do you think your survey results are similar to these, or different? Suggest reasons why this might be so.

3 Look at diagram **D** for Hereford. In what ways is it similar to or different from diagram **C**?

4 You have been asked by your council to produce a report comparing your town with the UK picture. Use the weblinks on the *Horizons* website to collect information about your town. You will need information on employment and unemployment, jobs, home ownership and health. You can add extra categories of information that you feel will support your report.

The report should present some information as graphs, maps and tables. **Remember:** if you use information you must explain it and compare it with the UK averages.

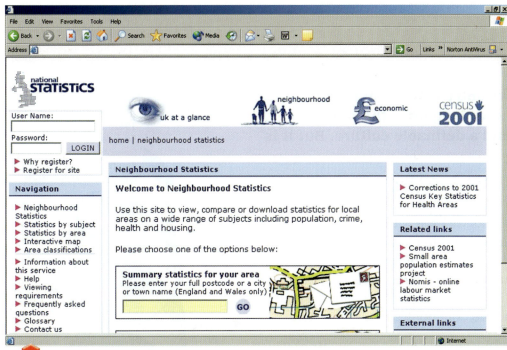

A Finding out about your town

B Finding out what people do in your town

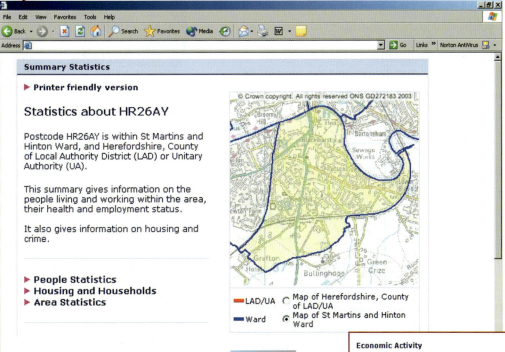

C The jobs people do in the UK

2%
20%
78%

KEY
Primary
Secondary
Tertiary

D The jobs people do in Hereford

6%
25%
69%

KEY
Primary
Secondary
Tertiary

Economic Activity

		Resident population aged 16 to 74 (percentage)	
	St Martins and Hinton	Herefordshire, County of	England and Wales
Employed	61.6	63.4	60.6
Unemployed	4.0	2.7	3.4
Economically active full-time students	1.7	1.9	2.6
Retired	13.7	16.1	13.6
Economically inactive students	2.2	2.9	4.7
Looking after home/family	6.9	6.2	6.5
Permanently sick or disabled	6.6	4.3	5.5
Other economically inactive	3.3	2.4	3.1

Source: 2001 Census, ONS

What links the UK with the world?

The United Kingdom is a country with borders, a government, a queen, its own language, the natural boundaries of an island and a definable culture. But it is not self-sufficient.

We buy many goods from abroad (**imports**) and must sell our goods and services abroad (**exports**) to pay for them. On pages 14–15 in Unit 1 you saw evidence of the links we have with the rest of the world, in one bedroom! You don't need to travel to realise that the UK has always depended on these links and has become what it is today through contact with other countries. The UK has links with every country in the world but especially close connections with the countries of the European Union (EU) and the Commonwealth.

The **European Union** is an organisation of European countries which encourages economic links. It also influences the laws of member countries and a wide range of social and environmental concerns. In early 2004, there were 15 countries in the EU. Ten more countries joined later in the year. Since the UK joined in 1973 it has enjoyed greater prosperity and more sustained economic growth than previously.

The **Commonwealth** is a group of nations, including the UK, which celebrates its common cultural links to support trade and development.

- It began when many former British colonial countries decided to maintain trade links with the UK and each other.
- It celebrates its unity at such important events as the Commonwealth Games.
- Many Commonwealth countries speak English as a first or second language.

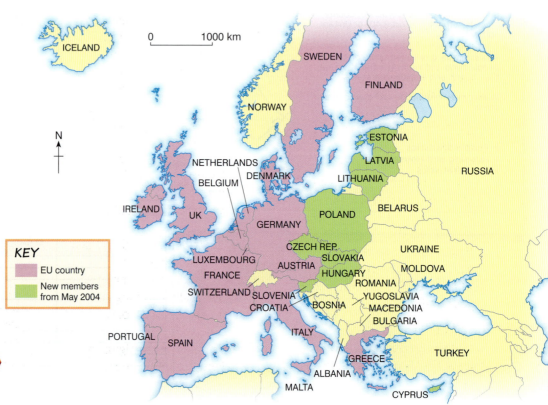

A Europe is getting bigger!

1957
Founder EEC members:
Belgium   Italy
France   Luxembourg
Germany   Netherlands

1973
Denmark
Rep. of
Ireland
UK

1981
Greece

1986
Spain
Portugal

1995
Austria
Finland
Sweden

May 2004
Cyprus   Lithuania
Czech Republic   Malta
Estonia   Poland
Hungary   Slovakia
Latvia   Slovenia

KEY
- EU country
- New members from May 2004

Members **B** of the EU

120

The UK will be able to trade more freely with other EU countries. That means a larger market for businesses to exploit.

We will get richer as the EU will bring more trade which will lead to a stronger economy.

The UK will follow EU laws on living and working conditions which will mean more help for the needy in our country.

We can all cooperate with each other to tackle issues like pollution, drugs, terrorism and refugees.

If all countries cooperate rather than pursue their own interests, we can make sure there is peace in Europe.

We will lose some of our powers to govern ourselves. We also lose the pound if we start to use the euro.

At least the UK government is democratically elected. Some important figures in the EU are not even elected.

The EU will impose its own laws and standards so we will lose part of our UK culture.

If we have better working conditions because of the EU, then UK industry will be less competitive than industry in other parts of the world.

When poorer Eastern European countries are allowed to join, it will drain money from wealthier countries like us!

C How European should the UK be?

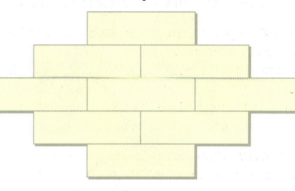

D Some of the 53 members of the Commonwealth

E Diamond 9 framework

Most important

Least important

---

1 a Using the information in diagram **A**, add labels to a copy of map **B**, to show the date when each country joined the EU. Do not label any countries that are not in the EU and are not intending to join.

  b Study your map. What do you notice about the location of the countries that joined the EU before 1975 and those that joined after 1975? (Useful words: *north, south, east, west, centre, core, edge.*) Write a sentence to describe your findings.

2 a Work in pairs. Study the following list of European links. On a copy of diagram **E**, arrange them in a diamond 9 formation to show which you think is most important.
  - Free health care on holiday
  - Able to work without a permit
  - EU football players in premier league
  - Ability to appeal to European Court of Human Rights
  - Subsidised road and bridge building
  - Grants for new industry and community projects
  - Education programmes
  - Support for farming and greater range of foods in our shops.
  - Frequent cheap flights to European destinations

  b When you have worked this out, compare your findings with those of the pair next to you or with the whole class. Which are the most highly prized links and which are the least valued?

  c i Colour in *green* those links that you think depend upon the UK being a member of the EU.
    ii Colour in *blue* those links that you think would exist even if we were not.

3 Look at cartoon **C** and then write a paragraph to explain why you think the UK should or should not be more integrated with the EU.

OVER TO YOU

121

UK tour

You now know a lot about the UK that visitors could benefit from. Not everyone wants the kind of UK tour that many companies offer. What should people see and why should they see it? How can they get to know the real UK?

A 'And on your left…'

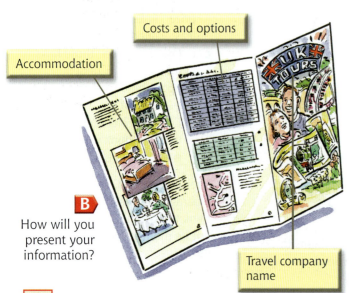

Accommodation

Costs and options

B

How will you present your information?

Travel company name

Help!

We may only understand what people in other countries think about the UK when we live and work with our neighbours more closely. Many of us have travelled, or will travel, to another EU country. The UK is likely to become more integrated with Europe in the future, and many of you will have the chance to work in other European countries.

OVER TO YOU

1 Design a five-day tour to show people *one* of the following:
   a what you consider to be the best of the UK
   b the *real* UK – the side the tourists never see
   c alternative UK, 'off the beaten track', e.g. a cycle tour.

Planning
A good tour has to be fully thought out. Think about the essentials:

meals

customers   transport   time allocations

cost   attractions   route   accommodation

options   recommended clothing/equipment

Put yourself in the tourists' shoes. Think of three questions you would ask about each of the above items before *you* would book the holiday.

Format
Your advertisement can be:
- a flyer
- a poster
- a storyboard for a commercial
- a video
- an audio-taped voice-over for a commercial
- a PowerPoint presentation.

Checks and balances
At each stage ask yourself if what you are planning gives a realistic, enjoyable experience and covers a good range of what the UK has to offer.

United Kingdom? Start here!

You have a good idea of what the UK is like, especially the part where you live. Now you are going to collect your file of information on the UK together ready to present it to the next set of Year 7 pupils. This will help them understand some of what you have already learned.

2 Skim-read through your file to remind yourself of the work you have done on the UK.

3 On an A4 page, draw a simple copy of the 'target' in diagram **C**. Using the categories on the diagram, follow these steps to fill the spaces:

   a Write down the most important features of the UK to you under each category.

   b Then try to add something about their characteristics (what they are like).

   c Then write why they are important in your view.

If you need to use more than four categories for the UK, make another copy of the diagram with more segments.

4 After you have completed your diagram, try to describe the links between at least one of the key characteristics in each section, on the back of the diagram or in your book, e.g.

WEATHER: *The weather is very changeable which makes farming difficult.*

WORK: *This is shown clearly in hilly areas like the Lake District.*

LANDSCAPE: *Here, the mountains can experience extremes of weather.*

PEOPLE: *Such weather conditions can cause danger to some visitors but offer opportunities to those on leisure pursuits.*

5 When you have finished, compare your target with that of a partner. Do you agree with their choice of the most important features? Explain your reasons.

6 Think about the ways in which:

   a learning a language

   b a common currency

   c cheaper and faster travel

could help you to get a job in the EU in the future.

1. Write down the most important feature to you under each category; e.g. 'UK people are varied.'

2. Then add a comment about the characteristics of this feature (what they are like); e.g. 'They belong to different countries and races.'

3. Then write why this is important in your view; e.g. 'This means they may have different languages, views and cultures.'

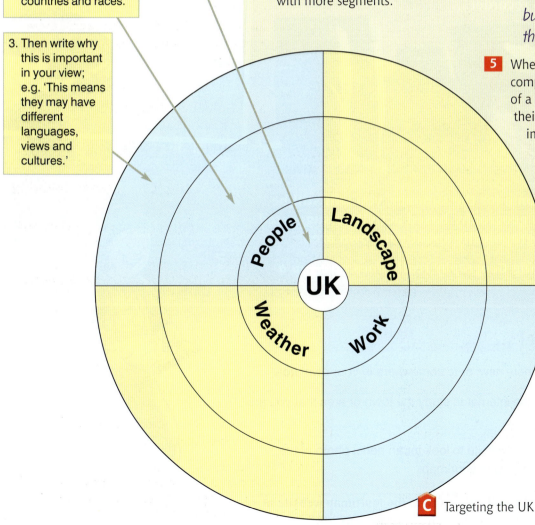

C Targeting the UK

PASSPORT TO THE WORLD

What is the geography of your holiday?

You've made it! You've reached the end of your first year of *Horizons*! We hope that you have enjoyed the journey, and that what you have learned has helped you all to become better geographers.

The summer break will be a chance to have a rest, and also to do some of the things that you miss during school term. You may be lucky enough to try new activities or even go to new places.

If you have started to think like a geographer, you will look at these new places with the eyes of a geographer... and you might think about them with the mind of a geographer... and then you might even create some geography with the skills you have learned, using your camera, pencils, video recorder...

If you are staying at home for the summer, you will still be able to do some of the geography-based activities suggested here, and to think geographically about your own area.

You will see that studying Geography really does give you a passport to the world!

Before you travel ...

Before you travel, to somewhere new, or to somewhere in your own area:

1 Download a map from the internet to study the town or area that you are visiting.

2 You can use the Multimap website to look for an aerial photo of the same place and compare it with your map.

WEBLINKS You will find a link to the Multimap website at
www.nelsonthornes.com/horizons/weblinks

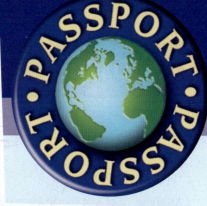

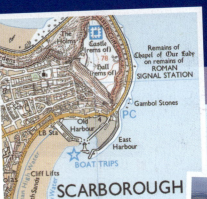

© Crown Copyright

SCARBOROUGH

While you are travelling ...

1 Plan your route on a map before you set out. Follow your route during the journey.

2 Notice the route of a bypass round a town. You might come across some of the points mentioned on pages 42-43.

3 Compare a railway route through a town with a road route through the same town. The railway often takes you through the old industrial area; roads often bypass the town but attract new industry to locate alongside them.

When you are there ...

Ask yourself the same questions that you thought about right back at the beginning of the year.

While you are there, keep thinking about these questions from time to time. You will find out more as you get to know the place better.

Send a postcard, showing the geography, back to your class.

- Where is this place?
- What is it like?
- Why is it like this?
- What do I feel about the place?
- How is it changing?
- Who is affected by these changes?

When you are back home ...

In a scrapbook, put together a collection of geographical images and information about the place you have visited, or make a wall display. Draw a map to show the places you have been to and the things you did there. Talk to your friends and ask them about the geography of their holidays.

Remember – you don't have to go far. There is geography on your doorstep!

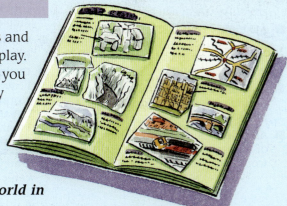

Geography gives you a passport that helps you to see the world in quite a different way as you travel through it.

Glossary

[Page numbers in *italics* indicate the first main reference in the text (no page numbers for 'How to' words)]

'How to' words

Analyse   Look at this in great detail. Try to see what has caused this place or thing to be like it is.

Annotate   Add notes around the map or sketch to explain the geography.

Compare   Look at two places together. Show how they are similar and how they are different.

Conclude   Make a final point to sum up what you think.

Describe   Say what you can see here (or what you can hear, touch, etc.).

Enquire   Find out all about.

Evaluate   Say how well something has been done. What were its strengths and weaknesses?

Explain   Give reasons for something.

Identify   Say what this is.

Interpret   Look carefully at something, then say what it means.

Investigate   Look into something very carefully and find out all about it.

Justify   When you have made a statement, give your reasons for it.

Summarise   Write a brief summing up of something, giving the main points.

Geographical words and terms

A

Abrasion   A river carries rocks and uses them to wear away at the river banks and bed.   *48*

Arable   Farming mainly growing crops like wheat and barley.   *91*

Assembly line   Often found in car plants. Each car moves along the line having more parts added by workers or by robots.   *95*

Assembly plant   A factory where components are put together to make finished products.   *95*

Attrition   A river carries fragments of rock, which rub together and get worn down.   *48*

B

Bias   Happens when someone tells only part of the truth. That person chooses only the bits that suit his or her own purpose.   *104*

Birth rate   The number of people born in a year – measured for every thousand of the population.   *30*

Boulder bar   A pile of boulders that has been deposited on the stream bed just below a waterfall.   *59*

British Isles   The group of islands that includes Great Britain and Ireland.   *107*

C

Capital intensive farming   Uses a lot of inputs of machinery, chemicals, etc. Produces big yields from a small area.   *90*

Cause   Something that leads to something else happening, e.g. heavy rain can cause floods.   *65*

Climate   The average of the weather over a period of many years.   *112*

Colony   A settlement that was started by people who moved into a new area.   *110*

Commonwealth   A group of nations with close cultural links, which supports trade and development.   *120*

Components   Parts. They are made in one factory and sent to an assembly plant to be made into finished products.   *95*

Condensation   Water vapour is cooled and turns back to water droplets.   *46*

Confluence   The place where a tributary joins the main river.   *47*

Cyclone   Very strong winds and heavy rain brought by a tropical storm. Cyclones occur in the Indian Ocean. They are called 'hurricanes' in other parts of the world.   *76*

D

Dairy farming   Mainly keeping cattle to supply milk.   *88*

Death rate   The number of people who die in a year – measured for every thousand of the population.   *30*

Dependents   The people in a country's population who are too old, or too young, to work.   *28*

Deposition   Fragments of broken rock that have been transported by rivers, etc. are dropped when the river loses energy.   *49*

Descendants   Someone's children, grandchildren, great-grandchildren ...and so on.   *110*

Doubling time   The number of years that it takes for a country's population to double.   *31*

E

Eastings   Lines on a map to show how far east you are. They run from north to south.   *6*

Effect   Happens as a result of something else, e.g. ruined carpets are an effect of floods.   *65*

Emigrant   Someone who moves away from a region or country.   *34*

Environmental geography   Study of the physical surroundings *and* the people, plants and animals that live there.   *8*

Erosion   Rock is broken up and carried away by moving water, ice or wind.   *49*

European Union   An organisation of European countries with close economic and political links.   *120*

Evaporation   Water is turned into water vapour, a gas.   *46*

Exports   Goods that are sold and sent out of the country.   *120*

Extensive farming   Uses a large area of land but only gives low yields. Often on poor land with a poor climate.   *90*

F

Flood   Usually when a river overflows its banks. It can also be caused by high sea level.   *65*

Flood plain   The area of flat land that is covered with water when a river floods.   *47*

Front A place where two types of air meet. Rain often falls at a front. *114*

Function What the settlement does. How it serves its people in the town and the surrounding area. *40*

G

Gorge A very narrow, steep-sided valley. *59*

Great Britain The biggest island in the British Isles. It contains England, Scotland and Wales. *106*

H

Human geography Where and how people live and work. *8*

Hydraulic action The weight and force of water in a river help to wear away at the river bed and banks. *48*

I

Immigrant Someone who moves into a new region or country. *34*

Impermeable A rock or other surface that will not let water pass through it. *67*

Imports Goods that are bought and then brought into a country. *120*

L

Labour intensive farming Uses a lot of labour to produce big yields from a small area. *90*

Land use How people use an area – for building, farming, industry, etc. *8*

Latitude Lines on a world map to show how far north or south a place is. *7*

LEDC Less economically developed country (poor) *32*

Longitude Lines on a world map to show how far east or west a place is. *7*

M

Mechanisation Where workers are replaced by machinery. *88*

MEDC More economically developed country (rich). *32*

Meteorology The study of weather. *112*

Migration The movement of people to another region or country to work and live. *34*

Mixed farming Has a mixture of crop growing and animals. *91*

Monsoon A weather season that brings very heavy rain to areas around the Indian Ocean. *76*

Mouth The point at which a river flows into the sea. *47*

N

Natural increase When the birth rate is higher than the death rate, natural increase is the extra population each year. *30*

Northings Lines on a map to show how far north you are. They run from east to west. *6*

O

Overhang Rock on a river side which has been undermined by river erosion. *59*

P

Pastoral farming Mainly grows grass to feed animals. *91*

Patterns In geography this means the way something is spread out over an area of land. *20*

Permeable A rock or other surface that will let water pass through it. *67*

Physical geography Natural features of the Earth, including landforms and the weather. *8*

Plunge pool A hollow in the bed of a river, formed where water plunges over a waterfall. *59*

Population density The number of people who live in an area of land. *26*

Population distribution The spread of people in an area. *24*

Precipitation Water droplets in clouds become too heavy and fall as rain, snow, hail, etc. *46*

Primary evidence Information that you collect yourself, usually by fieldwork. *18*

Primary industry or employment Produces raw materials from the land. Includes farming, fishing, forestry and mining. *84*

Process This is something that happens in an area and causes it to change. *44*

Prototype The first 'try-out' version of a new product. *97*

Pull factors Good things about a place that make people want to move there. *34*

Push factors Bad things about a place, which make people want to move away. *34*

R

Relief The height and slope of the land. *17*

River basin The whole area drained by a river and its tributaries. *47*

Run-off Water runs over the surface of the land. *46*

Rural An area in the countryside. *8*

S

Secondary evidence Information that you collect without visiting the place, from books, maps, internet, etc. *18*

Secondary industry or employment Work in a factory. Turns raw materials into finished products. *84*

Sediment Fragments of mud, sand and rock that have been dropped by a river. *60*

Site The land a settlement is built on. Ask yourself: 'Why was it built here, and not 500 metres away?' *38*

Situation How a settlement fits in with the wider region around it. *38*

Solar radiation Heat from the sun. *46*

Solution Some rocks – such as limestone – are dissolved and carried away by water. *48*

Source The place where a river begins to flow. *47*

Stereotypes Simplified views of people or places. They tell part of the truth but may be confusing. *108*

T

Tertiary industry or employment Does not produce 'things' but provides services for people. *84*

Throughflow Water flows through the soil. *46*

Total population All the people who live in one country. *26*

Transportation Broken rock is carried away by moving water, ice or wind. *49*

Tributary A smaller river that feeds into a larger river. *47*

U

United Kingdom A country that includes Great Britain and Northern Ireland. *104*

Urban An area in a town or city. *8*

W

Watershed High land, which divides the areas drained by two neighbouring river systems. *47*

Weather The conditions in the air around us – rain, wind, temperature, etc. *112*

Weathering Rock is broken up by frost, heat, chemical action, plant roots, etc. *48*

Index